Five Loaves and Two Bowls of Borscht

DISCOVERING GOD'S POWER IN UKRAINE

Janice Lemke

Purpose Press

Visit the Purpose Press website: www.purposepress.net
For more information about Christian Missionary Fellowship: www.cmfi.org

ISBN: 978-0-9845949-5-5

Thanks to Cory, my husband and partner in ministry.
I'm glad we're still friends.

Thanks to Janelle and Alicia, my daughters,
who added joy to the journey and (usually)
played nicely together while their mom was on the computer.

Thanks to Mom,
who was the first to encourage me to write.

Thanks to our friends in Ukraine;
this is their story too.

Thanks to the many who prayed
and therefore, share in the success.

Most of all, thanks to our Lord,
the author and perfecter of our faith.

Ukraine and Crimea

Contents

Prologue 7

1.   "Are We There Yet?".. 9

2.   "I Didn't Come Here for Adventure" 15

3.   The "Sink or Swim" Method...21

4.   Like a Trip to Disneyland...29

5.   Garlic and Pig Fat 39

6.   Garage Sale Paradise 45

7.   Off the Pedestal..53

8.   Walking in the Dark 59

9.   Rat Hats and Cough Syrup 69

10.   No Old Man on a Cloud 81

11.   He Is Risen Indeed 91

12.   Bitter Water Made Sweet 99

13.   Now What? 107

14.   Hope Endures 115

15.   We Battle Not Against Flesh and Blood 121

16.   Our Tiny Flame 129

17. "Always Ready" 135

18. Our Second Summer 141

19. "Don't Worry, It Will Get Worse" 147

20. Thankful for Candles 153

21. Heart Trouble 161

22. Training Begins 169

23. Village Visit 177

24. Camp and the KGB 183

25. "Blessed Inconveniences" 189

26. If You Don't Lose Heart 195

27. Graduation 201

28. Growing in Grace 207

29. Reap with Rejoicing 213

Afterward 217

Prologue

"So, how did you like it over there?" I hear this question often after my husband and I spent four years in Ukraine with our two little girls.

I battled with cockroaches in my kitchen and carried groceries from the local outdoor market. The entrance to our apartment building smelled like stale urine or worse. We had no hot water—and often, no water or electricity at all. I thought mission life is supposed to be exciting and fulfilling. Picking dead bugs from rolled oats isn't my idea of fun. It's depressing to live among people in despair.

"Life in Ukraine was more difficult than we expected," I answer, "but in the end, we saw more results than we anticipated."

We got to know two Christian men in the local Russian Evangelical Baptist Church who also wanted to see more people reached for Christ. Working together, we created a program to train men to start new churches in Eastern Crimea.

The Crimean Peninsula, home to 2.5 million people, lies south of mainland Ukraine and protrudes into the Black Sea. We estimate that less than one percent of the population regularly attends any kind of church. Most villages, even those with as many as 5,000 people, have no church of any kind.

The eleven men who entered the training program two years ago have started over twenty cell groups so far—potential churches. Many people have given their lives to Christ. The church planters are mentoring new believers, training them to start even more groups. Another thirty men recently began their training as church planters. Many of them have already started cell groups in towns without any previous church.

We can't claim credit for this; God has done great things. Our trials showed us our utter inadequacy. Nevertheless, God uses earthen vessels to accomplish His work. It's humbling to realize we would have missed out in the privilege of participation if we hadn't been willing to put up with a few cockroaches.

Our "good-bye" reception before leaving for Ukraine

-1-
"Are We There Yet?"

I held my two-year-old daughter, Alicia, with fingers locked together so she wouldn't fly off my lap. The van swerved back and forth on the narrow road, bouncing at each pothole the driver couldn't avoid. My husband, Cory, sat beside me and held Janelle, age three.

Janelle asked, "Are we there yet?"

It was July 30, 1995. We had traveled for over forty-eight hours since leaving the airport in Portland, Oregon. Upon arriving in Kiev, Ukraine, we boarded a train and headed south into the Crimean Peninsula. After seventeen hours on the train and two more hours in this van, we neared our final destination in Feodosia, a coastal town near the Black Sea.

I was ready to reach our new home too. I couldn't wait to wash off a layer of sweat and fine grit. I felt hungry and thirsty. The heat and humidity added to my misery. My body ached and my mind felt numb from the lack of sleep and so many new impressions.

"Yes," Cory assured Janelle, "we're almost there."

I saw row after row of gray, five-story apartment buildings as we passed through town. Though Feodosia had a population of around 80,000, we encountered only two stoplights. A crowded bus in front of us coughed black smoke from its tailpipe.

Sidewalks sustained a constant flow of pedestrian traffic. Old women wearing flowered scarves and faded housedresses shuffled along or stood chatting in small clusters. Some younger women looked like they had stepped from the pages of a fashion magazine with their miniskirts, high heels, and heavy makeup. A man in grubby clothes weaved unsteadily on his feet. Others walked around him. Almost everyone carried plastic shopping bags.

The apartment buildings of downtown Feodosia soon gave way to houses on the outskirts. Red tile roofs topped homes made of brick or stone and covered with crumbling plaster and whitewash. Bars covered windows. The houses sat close together, joined by stone walls that blocked our view of the inner courtyards.

Stefan* sat in the front seat of our van next to the driver. This Christian from Feodosia was a big man in his late 30s with a pleasant face and fair thinning hair. His wide smile revealed a gold tooth. I would later learn that gold teeth are common, but smiles are not.

Stefan had met us at the airport in Kiev and helped us get on the train. It had been such a relief to see him after we cleared customs. He greeted me with a firm handshake and Cory with a kiss. Russian Christians take seriously the admonition to "greet one another with a holy kiss."

Cory had met Stefan the previous year when he visited Feodosia with several church leaders from Kansas. Then he stayed just over a week. As a family, we planned to live in Ukraine for four years.

Our van climbed a steep hill and stopped in front of a sheet-iron gate painted blue. Stefan unlocked a door in the gate and began unloading our suitcases. We got out and followed him into a cement-covered courtyard.

To the left lay the house that had served as a church building. Stefan carried two suitcases to another building set further back on the property. That house had two rooms with a couple of beds in each. A third room contained a lumpy fold-down couch-bed, an old table, and several chairs. Faded yellow curtains hung from the windows. The place smelled musty but it looked clean.

Stefan took us outside again. I had seen pictures Cory had taken of the property when he attended church services here. This house and property once belonged to Stefan, but he had donated it to the church. Visitors from Kansas had stayed in this house.

When I asked those team members, "What is it like there?" they raved about the fantastic hospitality. "The church members were so loving," one said. "They treated us like family and fed us so well at every meal."

No banquet awaited us, however. Stefan took me to a small shed near the house. In the dim light, I saw open shelves along one wall. Cockroaches scurried over plates, enamel-covered pots, and silverware. The kitchen had no sink and no refrigerator.

Stefan showed me how to light the gas stove. "Ne rabotiet," he said, patting the oven. I understood—it doesn't work.

---

* Russian names have been changed.

I didn't know much Russian, but I felt grateful for the little I'd picked up in a night class before our move to Ukraine. We planned to spend the first year in Ukraine learning Russian. Instead of going to language school somewhere, we wanted to learn on-site, while building relationships.

Stefan showed us a cistern in the middle of the courtyard. He lifted the metal cover and grabbed a bucket with a rope attached. He threw the bucket into the cistern and pulled it up again, full of water. This would be our water supply.

I wished I knew more Russian. I wanted to ask Stefan, "How long will we be here? Have you looked for an apartment for us yet?" I told myself to go with the flow. I had no other choice.

"Zaftra," he said. Tomorrow. He pointed at his watch. At 10:00 he would take me grocery shopping. Then he left. We were on our own.

The place wasn't much, but I decided it would do, at least for a while. We had a good view of the Black Sea from the hill, and a nice breeze brought relief from the intense summer sun. I'd been camping before. It was far from the market, far from any store. There was no phone, no running water, and no refrigerator—but we wouldn't be there long. They would find us an apartment soon, or so we understood.

"Mommy," Janelle called urgently, "I've got to go pee-pee." Cory pointed to an outhouse. I took Janelle's hand and held my breath as I pushed open the door. There was no seat, just a hole in the cement floor about ten inches in diameter.

Janelle looked at the deep pit and shrieked, "No, no, I don't have to go."

I held her over the hole anyway. Nothing. "I don't have to go. I don't want to go," she screamed. I took her outside again. After much crying and dancing around, she finally used the seat-less outhouse.

We felt dehydrated after the long journey—hungry too. I didn't think we should drink the water, so I boiled it and made tea. We dined on crackers, dried fruit, and sausage—leftovers from our trip.

Linen sheets and faded bedspreads covered our beds. With the heat and humidity, we didn't need blankets. Cory and I put our thin, lumpy mattresses on the floor in the girls' room so we could be near them in this strange new place. Mosquitoes sang, but we soon fell asleep, exhausted.

I awoke around 3:30 a.m. and couldn't sleep again. The lumps in my mattress seemed more pronounced. Varmints above the ceiling scratched and scampered back and forth. I lay in the darkness and waited for morning. What had we gotten ourselves into?

I felt a bit like Abraham. I could identify with the description of him in Hebrews, "He went out, not knowing where he was going." He probably wondered how it would all turn out. He had seen God's faithfulness before, though, and I had too.

I used to think the worst thing God could do to someone is make him be a missionary. I was raised in the church and had seen many missionaries at Vacation Bible School and church camp. They were a strange species who wore funny clothes, ate weird food, told snake stories, and tried to get us to sing in a different language. I didn't want to be one.

Moving from the family farm in south-central Oregon to the University of Oregon in Eugene brought culture shock. Nevertheless, during those college years, I realized that being a Christian includes more than just going to church on Sunday—it requires that I live my life with the same priorities Jesus had. Jesus died for people, the type of sinful people I would rather ignore or avoid.

I started to work at a shelter home for delinquent or "throw-away" teens and grew to love those with a background very different from my own. A trip to Europe with my backpack the summer I turned twenty-one made the world seem smaller. Before that experience Europe seemed as far away as the moon, but I learned people are people everywhere, regardless of what language they speak.

My Bible readings revealed God's commitment to the peoples of the world. "Missions" isn't isolated in the "Great Commission" passage; it appears throughout the Bible. The Psalmist wrote, "Declare God's glory among the nations."

Yet, I felt inadequate. Could God really use me? I noticed how God used ordinary people in the Bible to do His work. I loved my family but read Jesus' words, "If you love father or mother more than Me you aren't worthy to be My disciples."

I still had reservations, like what about money? I didn't want to depend on others. I came from proud pioneer stock—we tried to be self-sufficient on the farm. God reminded me, "One part of the body can't say to another part, 'I have no need of you.'" The foot can't go anywhere if not attached.

God provided through others in the Body, and I didn't have to beg. I went to Kenya and worked with Youth With a Mission in Mombasa. I planned to stay for just two years, do my "good thing" for God, then come home and "be normal." I was ruined for the ordinary, however, and my two years stretched into five.

As I neared my thirtieth birthday in Kenya, I knew it was time to move on. I didn't know what God had next for me; I just knew it was time to return to Oregon.

Some of my Kenyan friends said, "Maybe the reason why God is taking you home is so you can get married." Maybe. Maybe not. I didn't want to go crazy looking.

Not long after my return, the pastor of my church in Klamath Falls introduced me to the congregation. After the service, a tall man with dark hair, brown eyes, and a mustache came up, introduced himself, and said, "It's nice to meet you. I've been praying for you."

Cory Lemke said he was interested in missions too and had read my newsletters. "I've never seen your picture though and assumed you were...well...ah, much more elderly. I feel so embarrassed." Not all single missionaries are old maids.

Cory had grown up in a mill town near Roseburg, Oregon and moved to Klamath Falls with his job at a power company. There, he met some Christians and gave his life to Christ at the age of twenty-one. He later felt God was calling him into the ministry, so he quit his job and went to Northwest Christian College (NCC) in Eugene.

His missions professor often said, "Never rule out cross-cultural ministry as an option for your life." Cory took the challenge and got a degree in missions. When I met him, he was working at NCC and taking masters classes in leadership development. He just happened to be visiting his home church the day I was introduced.

Cory returned to Klamath Falls two months later and invited me out for lunch. We started corresponding; he ran up his phone bill. God is a good matchmaker; we married fifteen months after we met. I think my parents must have sighed with relief when their adventurous, spontaneous daughter finally found a stable man with a more cautious approach to life.

I loved being married and making a nest. We had two children. Cory earned his master's degree. Our mutual interest in missions never died. We got excited about the possibility of ministry in Ukraine when Christian Missionary Fellowship sent us information about a new work they wanted to start there. We applied to work with them and they accepted us.

For over seventy years, the church in Ukraine had been repressed. With the breakdown of the Soviet Union, religious freedom existed once again. We wanted to help strengthen the church and train leaders in evangelism and church planting.

Where would we go in Ukraine? A large church in Wichita, Kansas had located a Russian Baptist congregation in Feodosia, which was open to partnership with an American church.

The Feodosia church said they needed a building in a more convenient location, so the Wichita church sent funds. They also sent short-term teams to help with evangelism. Seeing the need for an on-site missionary, they looked to our mission organization, CMF, for a recruit to Ukraine. We fit the bill.

We looked forward to our new life in Ukraine. The months spent raising support gave us friendships with people whose prayers would sustain us in the days ahead. I tried to prepare Janelle and Alicia for the move and told them, "First we will ride on an airplane a long way, then we will ride a train."

For months they asked, "When do we get to ride the train? I want to ride the train!" They had no idea what kind of adventures lay before us— none of us did.

Their long-awaited train ride was not as fun as they expected. Janelle wasn't the first one to be traumatized by a Ukrainian bathroom. When Alicia saw the ground whizzing by through the hole in the bottom of the dirty steel toilet, she too had cried, "I don't need to go! I don't need to go!" The train jerked and swayed. I braced against the wall and held her over the toilet anyway.

After months of preparation, we finally arrived in Feodosia. Our lofty goal of training leaders to plant new churches had been downsized to our own survival.

Train station in Kiev

- 2 -
"I Didn't Come Here for Adventure"

Day finally dawned with the sound of roosters crowing. From our perch on the hill, we could hear "Voice of Russia" broadcasting the morning news to sailors and ship engines droning in the harbor. The rising sun promised another hot day; it was already humid.

After more crackers, dried fruit, and sausage for breakfast, Stefan came to take me shopping at the large outdoor market downtown. We pushed our way through the crowd and surveyed long tables piled high with fruits and vegetables. I saw peaches, pears, cabbages, and tomatoes. The root crops—potatoes, carrots, and beets—still had soil attached.

In spite of the language barrier, Stefan and I soon worked out a system. He purchased and carried while I pointed out what I wanted. I felt overwhelmed by the crowd, the new language, and the new currency. Some day I would have to do this alone.

After buying produce, Stefan took me to the meat building where chunks of pork lay on the counter and hung from hooks. I knew it was pork by the pig's head sitting on the counter, staring lifelessly. I had no idea, though, how to tell which cut of meat would be good. Was it fresh? It smelled ok. The man behind the counter plopped another customer's purchase into a plastic bag and wiped his scale with a bloodstained rag. I wondered when he washed it last.

We finally stopped at the bread store where I found a great smell and more choices. I looked at round loaves, rectangular, oblong, dark bread, and light. I let Stefan choose.

I surveyed the groceries when I got home. Stefan had bought some amber-colored liquid in a two-liter pop bottle. Thirsty and thinking it was apple juice, I took a swig. It wasn't apple juice. It was sunflower seed oil!

Cory helped cut up the stew meat. Since we didn't have a refrigerator, I decided to boil it every morning and evening to keep it from going bad, until we ate it all.

Stefan came again the next morning, Sunday, to take us to church. The congregation was meeting in a rented hall downtown while work progressed on their new church building.

I had heard about the traditions of the Russian Baptist Church. Women must wear a head covering in church. "Good" Christian women don't wear makeup or jewelry. I wanted to show respect for the believers and fit in as best I could, so I donned my scarf and wore no makeup.

A few people greeted us when we arrived with a handshake or a kiss. The women kissed women in greeting, on the cheek or lips, and the men kissed men the same way. Most women wore long hair in a bun and covered it with a scarf. Some women smiled and nodded approvingly at my headscarf. I don't know what they thought about my short hair.

The pastor, Igor, knew a little English. "Welcome," he said, shaking Cory's hand. "I go now. I meet with Brothers." We had come to work with Igor and looked forward to getting to know him better. He was one year younger than Cory, but he looked older with his serious expression, receding hairline, and graying hair.

Our most enthusiastic welcome came from a woman with short brown hair, makeup, and no headscarf. "Menya zavut Anya," she said with a big smile. "Anya," she repeated, patting her chest. "I...love...you," she said slowly in English with a heavy accent. She ushered us to a seat and sat down beside us.

The service began with prayer, then singing. Anya shared her hymn book with me and pointed out the words. I had learned the Russian alphabet and a few phrases but understood little other than "Amen" at the end of prayers. I stood and sat on cue with everyone else. My sense of isolation gave me more incentive to learn Russian so I could understand and communicate. These people were my new family; we had no one else.

The two-hour service included three sermons, interspersed with songs, prayers, and poems. The room felt stuffy, and heat accented the smells of honest work and garlic. It didn't take long before Alicia started wiggling and fussing. Anya fished around in her purse and brought out a small makeup mirror and a pocket-sized Bible, which she gave Alicia and Janelle for entertainment. The novelty quickly wore off, so I took them outside.

We found quite a few children playing in the cement-covered courtyard. Janelle and Alicia watched but weren't ready to join them. One of the teens tried to teach me "Jesus Loves Me" in Russian, but my mind was foggy from lack of sleep, and I couldn't remember anything.

People back home still didn't know we had arrived without mishap. We brought a laptop computer to Ukraine and hoped to quickly get hooked up on e-mail. Sunday afternoon, Cory went with Igor and Stefan to take care of this but had no success. Our first lesson in Ukraine: nothing will be as easy as you think it should be.

We tried to bring only the basics from America. I figured that people in Ukraine cook with something and eat off something, so why bring the extra weight of pots, pans, and dishes? My kitchen shed had enamel covered pots but no fry pan. It took us weeks to find one.

Our second lesson: learn to make do. I had brought a cookie sheet, which became a substitute. The eggs we got at the market were old, and the bread was stale by the next day. Together they made good French toast. Sugar, water, and American maple flavoring made good syrup.

After breakfast, we washed clothes. Cory pulled water up from the cistern in a bucket. I heated it on the old gas stove. While I scrubbed clothes in a huge enamel-covered pot, Cory rinsed and hung them on the line. Janelle and Alicia wanted to help too—wanted to play in the water, anyway. The job didn't take very long as a family affair.

Stefan came to take me shopping again. After we bought more produce at the open-air market, he took me to a grocery store for flour. He gave the woman behind the counter a plastic bag. She scooped flour from a large gunnysack and weighed our purchase on her scale. Stefan turned to me and pointed to a stack of small tin cans on a shelf behind the counter. Then he made the motion of spreading something on his other outstretched hand. *Great*, I thought, *I found some margarine, or maybe it's jam. It will be good to have something on our bread at last.* I nodded my head.

Opening the can later, I found some kind of fish spread—brown and pasty. "It looks like cat food," Cory said. I served it for lunch anyway. It tasted strong and salty, but was edible with a tomato slice on top. Lacking refrigeration, I spread it on thick trying to use it up.

Between the outhouse and main house stood a small outdoor shower. It had three walls and a door but no roof. I felt safe taking a shower under the sky—until I heard voices on the hill above us. Though the water tank above the spigot was heated by the sun, I decided to shower at night or crouch down low.

By Tuesday, Cory and I felt quite isolated up on the hill. We had no contact with anyone from the church unless they came to visit us. We felt helpless. We didn't know how to walk to any stores. We didn't know where anyone lived and had no phone. We still hadn't made contact with home. We wondered about progress toward finding an apartment..

I finally got a good night's sleep, though, so I felt ready to explore. "Do you want to go for a walk?" I asked Cory.

"No, I'll stay here," he replied. "I didn't come to Ukraine looking for adventure."

"Ok, but I've got to get out. Come on girls, let's go for a walk." I took Janelle and Alicia by the hand.

"Be careful," Cory called as I stepped outside.

Instead of taking the longer road, we headed straight down the hill, walking on a rocky path. I felt disappointed Cory didn't join us on this outing, but I accepted our differences. He's a "look-before-you-leap" kind of guy. I just jump in and figure out later what I got myself into. He worried about our safety, but I wondered how he would adapt in a country where so much lay out of his control.

I had asked him once, "Why can't you be more spontaneous?" He replied, "I don't know, I'm just not that way." Fortunately, he never asked me, "Why aren't you more organized?" We had our own strengths and worked well together as a team.

The girls and I met four goats coming up the hill, snatching at tufts of grass as they came. A thin old woman wearing a tattered gray dress followed them, carrying a long stick. The smallest goat chose Alicia as a playmate for a game of tag. As he hopped towards her, she began to scream. I picked her up and tucked Janelle behind me. The old woman beat her goat into submission.

The path ended and we followed potholed pavement and cobblestone past old stone houses with crumbling plaster. Chickens scratched through compost piles. Stray dogs wandered and skinny cats sunned themselves. Old women in faded housedresses worked in small gardens or watched small children play with sticks and dirt. The tots wore nothing more than gray underwear and sandals.

At the foot of the hill, I found a row of women selling garden produce in front of a grocery store. I had seen this place from the car and felt proud of myself for finding it.

After our solitary confinement on the hill, I wanted to make contact with people. I knew the words for "how much does this cost" and "write it down please." I didn't have any money, but it seemed like a good opener. I approached the woman selling tomatoes. I learned her name was Vera, but didn't understand anything else she said.

I inspected the shop. The store stretched for half a city block but contained less than an American mini-mart. All goods lay behind a long wooden counter. One section sold different kinds of bread. Mid-counter I found plastic containers of macaroni, unknown grains, hard candy, and coarse salt. A display case contained salami sticks, cheese, chunks of pork fat, and milk in half-liter bottles. Jars of pickles and cans of unknown content occupied shelves behind the counter.

Each new day was like opening one of those mystery cans. The next morning, a man from the church named Andre came at 6:00 a.m. to take us to Melitopol. Our teammates, Steve and Jo Laine Wright, lived in this town four hours north of us with five-year-old Cameron and teenage Carmen. They had come to Ukraine eight months earlier and were still learning Russian. We looked forward to spending the next four days with them and learning what we could about how to cope in this foreign land.

Our driver, Andre, a sandy-haired man in his mid 30s, had a slim athletic build. His expression was hard to read—he neither smiled nor scowled, just watched as though taking everything in. We had heard about Andre before. A friend in Kansas had told us, "Andre looks so serious he reminds me of a KGB agent. He's a great Bible teacher, though."

Andre had started a Bible study for new believers after a team from Wichita held evangelistic meetings in Feodosia. Older church members came to hear Andre's teaching too. They tried to pass on their legalistic traditions, and the new believers slowly stopped coming.

Andre knew a little English and taught us some Russian words as he drove. He pointed out communal farm villages and told us the workers there earned only $10 per month. Factory workers typically earned $40 per month. When we stopped at an outhouse, Janelle exclaimed, "We have a hole like this!"

Steve and Jo Laine welcomed us and showed us around their apartment. I hoped we could get one like it. "Someone in the church found it for us right after we got here," Steve said. "The people who own it immigrated to Israel. It was already furnished. We just had to buy a few things. We really like it."

The Wrights came to Ukraine to work with a fast-growing newer congregation. The church welcomed them, but life had still been difficult. We listened to their struggles, prayed together, discussed language learning, and used their e-mail. We enjoyed the American fellowship and indoor toilet. The girls played with five-year-old Cameron and watched videos.

On our second day with them, a doctor diagnosed Cameron's skin infection as highly contagious. Other children in his kindergarten had similar sores. We shortened our stay and returned to Feodosia early.

Like our teammates, we planned to spend the first year of our four-year term learning Russian. Our mission organization emphasized that we must not jump into ministry right away. We also believed our work would be more effective if we learned the language first.

Nevertheless, when Igor asked Cory to preach on our second Sunday in Feodosia, he agreed. He wanted to let people know why we came. Using an interpreter, he spoke about the importance of every member of the Body of Christ using his or her gifts for the extension of the Kingdom. He reminded them of the 80,000 people in Feodosia without Christ. A town this size should have many churches, just like it has many bread stores where people go for fresh bread. The Tatars, a Muslim people group, also need to know Christ.

We didn't know it at the time, but we later learned that the church leaders were certain we had come to split the church. They had seen Americans do that in other towns. We simply wanted to see the church growing and reaching out instead of hiding behind church walls. Many years of oppression had taught believers to keep to themselves and encouraged suspicion of outsiders.

On hill above our first house, overlooking the Black Sea and Feodosia's old fort

- 3 -
The "Sink or Swim" Method

We wanted to build relationships while learning the language, so we studied the LAMP (Language Acquisition Made Practical) method before coming to Ukraine. The idea behind this technique is to learn a few phases daily and practice them with the local people. A variation of it worked for us, but we renamed it "the sink or swim method."

During our second week in Feodosia, we began meeting with our language helper, Tatiana. She worked at an art gallery and had translated for American teams who visited the Feodosia church. She agreed to come to our house on the hill three times a week. "It's only a thirty-minute walk from my house," she said. I learned later it was much further for her, more like an hour.

I liked Tatiana right away. She wasn't a believer, but she had a kind face and a pleasant personality. She spoke and carried herself with an air of quiet dignity.

Though we lived in Ukraine, people around us spoke Russian, not Ukrainian. On our first day, we focused on learning, "Hi, my name is Janice (Cory.) I am learning Russian. Can I practice my Russian with you? Thank you. Good bye." The unfamiliar pronunciation made a terrible mouthful. Tatiana made a tape of the words in Russian so we could listen to them over and over.

We were supposed to form a language route made up of people with whom we could practice new phrases every day. Tatiana cautioned us, "Don't be surprised if people don't want to talk to you. During the Cold War, there were posters around town which said, 'Keep Silence.' We were told that anyone could be a spy, and we shouldn't talk to strangers. Besides that, life is hard these days and people are more rude."

Though I never developed a proper language route, I found old women who were willing to chat, especially if I had Janelle and Alicia along. Old ladies often commented on the "cute little girls" and gave them flowers or tomatoes from their gardens.

We also had contact with people from the church. Olga, Pastor Igor's wife, came over one day to teach me how to make borscht. Since I didn't have carrots or beets, she went next door to borrow some for this poor American. She chopped up the onions, and then searched around my kitchen. I finally understood she wanted a frying pan. I showed her my cookie sheet. Unimpressed, she chose an enamel-covered pot instead. Her two little boys played with Janelle and Alicia while we cooked.

Since Olga knew no English, our conversation was minimal. While our borscht boiled, I showed her photos of family and home. I knew enough Russian to point out family members, "Mama, Papa, Sistra, Brat."

I walked her to her house, about twenty minutes away, so I would know how to get there. She showed me her photo album, full of pictures of solemn faces in black and white.

Our need to eat gave opportunities to practice Russian. After returning from Olga's, I went to buy bread at the shop at the foot of our hill. I pointed out the loaf I wanted. The clerk pulled the appropriate bills from my bundle. I stared at the cans behind the counter and wondered if one of them was jam. Maybe one with a plum on it? *I'll ask another time*, I thought. *No customers at the milk counter...I'll practice my Russian there.*

The clerk stood chomping on bread and salami, talking with another worker. I asked for kefir. I already had some of this thin yogurt at home, but at least I could pronounce it and it made good pancakes. I pointed at a yellow block, which looked like butter and hoped that's what I'd get. *Just a small amount*, I motioned. She weighed my purchase on a scale.

At the far end of the store, I found blankets. We would need some before winter. I asked a woman behind the counter for the price and gave her a paper to write her answer. Over three million – $20 – half a month's salary for most people. I wondered how local people could afford it.

I scanned the produce outside looking for eggs. The meat we kept re-boiling must have made us sick. Eggs stay fresh longer, but I had bought eggs on their deathbed, too. I saw no eggs, so tried to buy carrots. The lady wrote: 15,000. Just ten cents U.S. After my purchase, she told another woman the price was 12,000. *Oh well*, I thought, *so I paid two cents extra ...not a bad price for learning to get around in Russian.*

I decided I must learn the numbers, not just one through ten, but hundreds of thousands. With Ukraine's run-away inflation, one US dollar was worth 150,000 Ukrainian coupons. The smallest bill was 500 coupons, worth less than one cent US. It didn't take much to be a millionaire.

Shortly before we moved to Ukraine, I wrote an enthusiastic letter to a friend, a former missionary. Laurie wrote back, "I remember how it is, you can't wait to get to the mission field; then you get there and wonder why you ever came." I dismissed the comment as part of her negative experience. I was sure I would never feel that way.

Two weeks after arrival in Ukraine, I wrote in my journal:

I'm covered with bug bites and my intestines churn. I'm tired of camping and want an indoor bathroom and a refrigerator. I can't even engage in small talk, much less expound the great truths of Scripture to a lost and needy world. I feel as powerful and competent as a small piece of driftwood in the surf.

Why did we come anyway? We came because people in Ukraine are important to God. Jesus could have stayed in heaven where it was comfortable, but He left His place of privilege to come to this sin-sick world.

I feel helpless and don't like it. I can't talk to people, get to know them or express my desires. We can't find an apartment on our own and still don't know our way around town. We are dependent on other people to help us.

Though Jesus existed in the form of God, with all power, He came as a helpless baby. Did that helplessness frustrate Him? I don't think so. He was humble, willing to wait. Even as an adult, His power was limited—at least He limited the way He used it. He could have called legions of angels to ease His situation, but He didn't.

We were often sick during our first month. Still, I had to roll out of bed to make breakfast, wash clothes, buy groceries. Stefan took me shopping in his car once a week, but lacking refrigeration, I hiked twenty minutes down the hill for perishables. The woman selling bread scolded me once for not having correct change. At least she seemed angry—I couldn't understand what she said.

The language barrier heightened my sense of isolation. Even in my dreams I was an outsider, trying to join a group without success. I felt self-conscious, but had to be willing to make mistakes in order to practice Russian.

With intestines in turmoil, we ran to the outhouse often. The girls needed an adult to hold them over the hole so they wouldn't fall in. I got calls in the night, "MOMMY, I've got to go to the bathroom!! Carry me! Hurry!"

I came home one day from shopping and collapsed on the bed. "Will you read to us?" Janelle gave me one of the books we had brought from Oregon. I was too tired to get up, so she and Alicia crawled in bed with me. I had read the book many times already, but began again.

The story featured a raccoon named Adam and a king lion who represented Jesus. Adam thought he could figure out how to run the race his own way, without following the map. He got lost, wasted time, became tired, and was ready to give up. The lion came and got him back on track. Run the race with your eyes on me, the king urged. I've run it before and I will be with you every step of the way.

My eyes flooded with tears when I read the lion's words of encouragement. I needed that reminder.

Tatiana taught us more than Russian. She showed me how to walk downtown where I could peruse the shops. She identified what was in some of those mysterious jars and cans. Jars contain cabbage something and tomato something and cans hold different kinds of fish and meat. She helped us find a fry pan.

She provided a wealth of knowledge about the town we lived in. "Feodosia is an ancient town," she explained. "It was founded by the Greeks 500 years Before Our Era."

"You mean 'Before Christ?'" I asked. Apparently, they didn't use that term in English classes in Soviet schools.

She continued, "The Greeks named the town, 'Theodosia,' meaning 'Gift of God.' Our region became a major source of slaves and grain. Some say the Apostle Andrew stopped here on one of his missionary journeys."

She pointed out a large park at the foot of our hill, near the store I had found. "This was the slave market. Feodosia had the largest slave market in Europe. Slaves were sold here over a period of 2,000 years. They went to Greece and later Turkey and various Arab nations. Historians say that as many as 30,000 slaves were available for sale at a time." I later heard that the word "slave" came from "Slav," because Slavic peoples were used as slaves.

I found old fortress ruins near the sea on one of my exploratory walks with Janelle and Alicia. Cows grazed in a valley between a fortress wall with turrets on one side and ancient stone buildings on the other. The shimmering Black Sea lay in the background.

"We have that picture in a book," Janelle said. It did look like a scene from a storybook.

The ancient stone buildings were old churches. One had no doors so we went inside. We saw crosses carved in stone over the rounded doorway and remnants of paintings on the domed ceiling. Graffiti marked the walls. Broken bottles and other trash littered the floor. It smelled of urine.

Janelle said, "I'm sad the church is broken." I was too.

Tatiana told us later the church was built in the 14th century. She also told us about the fortress. The Tatar (related to the Mongols) ruled the region when Genoese (Italian) merchants came by ship early in the 14th century. The merchants asked the Tatar ruler about the possibility of buying a piece of land here. The ruler said they could buy as much land as they wanted, as long as they covered that land with cow skin and covered the hide with ten layers of gold coins. The merchants took a cow skin, covered it with gold coins, and cut the hide into very thin strips, almost threads. They tied the threads together and used it to mark out the territory. The Tatar admired their ingenuity and gave them the land.

When building a fortress for their town, the Italians mixed egg white in the mortar, making a strong stone wall. The town became a busy trading center, a transfer point for spices, silk, china, and other goods headed to Europe from the East. The Black Plague also entered Europe through Feodosia's port in the 14th century and killed one third of Europe's population. The old part of Feodosia, where we lived, is still called "Quarantine" to this day.

I found Tatiana's history lessons fascinating. Knowing I lived in an interesting place lightened the sense of drudgery I felt in tedious tasks. I wondered if Christopher Columbus, also from Genoa, visited this port on a merchant ship before seeking a shortcut to the East. He could have.

Tatiana said the old mosque near the former slave market was built in the 14th or 15th century. In the 1970s, city officials restored the building and opened it as a museum. Many people came for a special exhibition, but the floor sank slightly, so authorities closed the building again. They discovered a tunnel under the floor, which they believe leads to the sea, but lack of funds prevented further excavation.

Feodosia once had many churches, but times changed. Tatiana told us her grandfather studied to become an Orthodox priest in the early 1900s—just so he could marry a certain woman who was the daughter of a priest. After he went through many years of religious training and won his bride, the Revolution took place and the new leaders closed most churches. He went back to school to become a teacher.

Tatiana's grandmother kept her religious ways. From Grandma, young Tatiana picked up terms such as "Lord!" to express surprise. Her schoolteachers rebuked her, "Do not use outdated words that have no meaning." She learned to hide the fact that she had a religious family member.

Though teachers tried to erase the influence of Christianity, they could not change the Russian language. The word for Sunday means "resurrection." The word for Saturday sounds like "Sabbath." The word for "thank you" means, in Old Russian, "May God save you."

Tatiana said she had a Bible and reading it gave her comfort, especially parts of the Old Testament. She took her Bible to the hospital when she had a minor surgery and read it to some other patients. She wasn't sure what to think about the New Testament, though.

We wondered how people like Tatiana would fit in at the church, especially after a visit from two college-age girls. Since they spoke English, we could talk freely. They came wearing pants, makeup, and jewelry. They had accepted Christ two years earlier and seemed excited about their faith. We asked them about the openness of young people to Christianity.

"People are open to talking about God and truth," said one, "but they don't want to join the church because of the traditions and legalism. You hear a lot of rules at church, like you're not supposed to wear makeup and jewelry."

Feodosia's old fortress and 15th C. church

Washing dishes by the cistern

We bought produce at an outdoor market

A 15ᵗʰ C. Turkish mosque being restored for use

- 4 -
Like a Trip to Disneyland

Weeks passed, and we still had no apartment. I didn't like depending on other people for phone and transportation. It was inconvenient to them and to us, but our reliance gave us contacts and relationships we might not have built otherwise.

We rejoiced to finally get an e-mail account, but Cory had to carry our laptop computer to Giorgi's house, a twenty-minute walk away, to use the phone. Giorgi managed a shoe factory. His home was small and simple, but he was one of the few church members with a telephone.

The girls and I walked to his house with Cory one day. We hiked up and down small hills passed grazing goats and old stone houses. The girls liked our family outing—Alicia especially liked Daddy's strong arms, which carried her when she got tired.

Giorgi's wife, Luba, met us at the door, ushered us into their bedroom and pointed to a couch. We sat down. Giorgi moved a small, wooden end table away from the wall and transformed it into a longer guest table by raising the flaps and bracing them in place. Luba took matching teacups from the china cabinet near us, wiped them with her dishtowel, and set the table. We had just dropped in, but they treated us like special guests.

Luba served tea and bread with homemade jam and later pulled out their photo album. Giorgi had several sisters in the church, including Olga, Pastor Igor's wife. His father had been a church elder, but he died the previous year after a car hit him.

Janelle and Alicia liked playing with Giorgi and Luba's five children. The oldest climbed a plum tree in the garden to pick snacks. Janelle and Alicia inspected the chickens and sheep penned in a corner of their small back yard. Alicia took charge of their kitten and ate too many plums.

After Giorgi learned we had no refrigerator, he brought us an extra one he had. A tiny, old refrigerator never looked so good! I wouldn't have to worry about our food spoiling!

When Tatiana heard about it, she thought our enthusiastic response was funny. "I told my husband, 'These Americans have such simple tastes. They are so happy with a refrigerator and a fry pan.'" After being without we really did appreciate the simple things.

I often thought of advice I'd heard from a missionary to Russia, "Look at each day as a trip to Disneyland. It will take the edge off of not knowing what to expect."

This advice came in handy while shopping. One day, I went to the nearest shop for bread. They didn't have any. "When will you have bread?" I asked.

I couldn't understand the answer. As I stepped outside, I saw the bread truck pull up. I waited a long time for the clerk to count the loaves and finally got one.

We continued to wait for the promised apartment, but Stefan and Igor said they couldn't find one big enough and with a telephone. They found smaller apartments, but we didn't want to sleep in the living room. I was tired of camping and wanted a few more amenities. I knew how to walk to town, but the long trip left me exhausted.

We had been in Ukraine one month when we had an American over for dinner. He was the only other missionary in town and worked with the new charismatic church. Among other things, we talked about our need for an apartment.

Two days later, he came puffing up the hill. "I told my pastor you need an apartment," he said. "He found you one this morning."

Cory went to look at it and came back with a glowing report. "You'll love it," he told me. "It's close to the center of town. It's near the market and post office, and it's upstairs from a grocery store. It doesn't have any furniture, but we can get some."

The next day, Cory took the girls and me to see the place. Igor came too, to negotiate with the landlord. As we ascended the dirty, graffiti-marked stairwell to the fourth floor, I tried to stay positive.

The landlord unlocked the door and ushered us into a tiny entryway. Cory began his tour. "Here's the bathroom," he said, pointing out a stall with a toilet only. The open door next to it revealed a small washroom with a tub and sink. Then we stepped into the kitchen.

I stood in a daze in that tiny room. Other than a small sink and an old gas stove, there was nothing else. No shelves, no cupboards, nothing. Where would I put plates or food? I stared at the limestone walls. Was it even possible to attach cabinets to these walls, if we could find cabinets? I stared at a bare wire hanging from the ceiling where a light fixture should have been. I had been excited about moving downtown but now realized the apartment needed much work before we could move in.

"Come on," Cory urged. "Come and see the rest of the house." I went back toward the entryway and turned right through another door.

I walked over rough floorboards painted mustard-brown. Off the main room were doors to two smaller rooms. The smell of fresh paint filled the air. New white gloss around windowsills was still sticky and covered ancient layers that were cracked and peeling. Cheap wallpaper hid limestone walls. There were no shelves anywhere. No closets for our clothes. No curtains or curtain rods.

"What do you think?" Cory asked.

"It will take a lot of work..."

"I know, but we haven't found anything else. We can get furniture. I'll fix it up. The landlord is waiting. He has already drawn up a contract."

At least it has a phone, I told myself. And an indoor toilet...and a balcony where I can hang laundry...and it's closer to the market.

While Cory and Igor met with the landlord and the girls played in empty rooms, I slipped outside to see the courtyard. There were trees but no grass—just weeds and dirt. Dingy gray linens hung on the clothesline. A housewife beat a rug draped over a bar. Metal steps to a slide ended in the air, with no slide attached. A few children climbed on rusty monkey bars. Several park benches had legs but nothing to sit on. We were moving to the slum.

I talked little that evening. As I lay in bed that night staring into the darkness, hot tears ran into my ears. I didn't like that apartment at all. Other missionaries I knew in Ukraine moved into furnished apartments. I expected to find some cozy place lacking only occupants. It wasn't Cory's fault; he was doing his best to improve our situation. I was so tired of simply coping with life, I couldn't imagine finding the energy needed to get that apartment livable.

Having grown up in the U.S., I was used to more options. Americans look at several houses before choosing one. I felt like a bride in a country where marriages are arranged. Such a bride has no choice—no choice but to choose her own happiness and to choose to make it work.

"God," I prayed, "I know that in Your presence is fullness of joy and at Your right hand are pleasures forever more. Help me find my peace in You. Help me make this apartment a home and a place of peace."

I needed grace to get through this, I realized. God gives grace to the humble. Perhaps my point of pride is thinking I deserve to have life a bit more comfortable than the average Ukrainian.

"Lord, help me be more like You. Self dies a painful death. I already have it easier than the average Ukrainian and many others in the world. I don't have to watch my children go hungry and wonder what I will feed them. We have money for food and furniture. Thank you for answering our prayers and providing an apartment with a telephone in a more convenient location."

The American pursuit of happiness is largely consumer oriented, I realized. Not happy? Then get a different brand, a different spouse, a new house, or more stuff. I remembered seeing a documentary film about Russian immigrants in the U.S. They felt overwhelmed by so many choices. In Russia, they didn't ask themselves if they are happy or not— they just did their best with the circumstances they had. I would have to learn to do the same.

Over the next few days, Cory and Igor purchased furniture and hauled it up four flights of stairs. The kitchen cabinets and wardrobe required assembly. Ukrainian homes typically have freestanding wardrobes instead of built-in closets. They bought beds, a table, pans, and a mirror.

I appreciated Igor's help and Cory's efforts to make the house a home. I didn't have the energy to help pick out furniture, but Cory said there wasn't much to choose from anyway.

While Cory worked at the apartment, I prepared for our move. I put laundry to soak in buckets and went inside to sweep the house. I heard a blood-chilling scream and ran outside. Alicia was crying.

"All right, Janelle," I demanded, "tell me what happened." Alicia tried to give the neighbor's cat a bath, and the cat didn't like it.

On moving day Igor came to get our few belongings and us. Cory had done a good job assembling cupboards and closets. The kitchen looked much more useable. The floors were still ugly but not quite as rough as I remembered.

Anya came to help us mop floors and get moved in. She was the woman with short hair and makeup who sat beside me on our first day in church and had given candy to the girls every Sunday since then. She lived nearby and brought us a pot of borscht for lunch. When praying for an apartment, we had prayed for good neighbors. God knew what He was doing after all.

Anya became a good friend to us. She lacked the reserve typical of most Russians or Ukrainians and was pushy enough to be the kind of friend I needed. Most people feel awkward or impatient trying to talk to someone who doesn't know the native language. Not Anya—she found ways to overcome the language barrier. Though she worked at the post office, she once taught elementary school and knew how to speak simply. When words failed, she used mime.

She came over our first morning and said something about milk. I didn't understand, so she grabbed my two-liter kettle with a bucket handle and told me to come with her. She led me to a truck with a big tank parked outside our apartment building. A woman wearing a white scarf and white apron dipped milk from a big metal container and filled the jars and pans brought by housewives. She filled her big pot from a hose on the back of the truck. The milk came from a collective farm and cost less than half the price of bottled milk at the store. I took the milk home and cooked it.

Anya invited me to bring the girls over that morning, so it seemed like a good time for Cory and me to look at furniture in local shops. We planned to be gone just an hour but didn't know how to say the whole sentence in Russian.

"One hour," Cory simply told her.

We found a gray couch and matching chairs. By choosing our own furniture, we weren't stuck with brightly-colored, mismatched pieces that clashed with the wallpaper and curtains.

When we returned, Anya and the girls weren't home. We worried until we realized that "one hour" and "one o'clock" sound the same in Russian, at least to us. Still I kept an impatient watch until Anya brought the girls back a little after 1:00. She had taken them to see the Black Sea and a snake exhibit, and then bought them ice cream. The girls had fun while Mom was having a fit.

A few days later Anya took me to the sea, a mere five-minute walk away. We headed up the busy street by our apartment. The smell of diesel fumes filled the air as trucks, buses, and cars roared down the two-lane, one-way road. Several kiosks sat in the shade of a five-story apartment building: one sold bread, another, music cassettes. A third booth featured soap products and cosmetics. At the stoplight, one of the few in town, we crossed the road and walked down a pedestrian street. Along this block, we passed sidewalk cafes with round tables under big umbrellas that advertised Marlboro cigarettes or Coca-Cola. American rock music blared from loudspeakers at each cafe.

During summer months, several trainloads of Russian tourists arrived daily into Feodosia, so the area around the beach was as crowded as an American shopping mall before Christmas. Oil paintings of landscape and sea leaned against a building, guarded by artists who hoped to sell them. Portrait artists sketched and painted tourists posing for a more personal souvenir.

Along the beach lay a wide promenade designed to keep winter storms at bay. It was made of huge cement blocks and covered with more decorative bricks. Vendors displayed their wares along this walkway: sunglasses and sunflower seeds, trinkets made with shells or wood, homegrown fruit, and slices of multi-layer cake. Photographers with monkeys and plastic palm trees offered to take our picture.

We looked over the iron railing to the pebble-covered beach about eight feet below. Colorful towels and sunbathers in various shades of bronze or pink covered the beach. Some vacationers played and swam in the gentle waves. The water didn't seem very clean to me and had big patches of seaweed. I found the scene interesting, but since I don't like crowds and don't like to sunbathe, I didn't feel tempted to run home for a beach towel.

When Sunday came, Anya showed us the way to church. The congregation had just moved into their new facility. The remodeled house was ready for worship services, but more work was needed to finish a separate building with a kitchen and rooms for Sunday School.

With the weather warm, children met outside for Sunday School. They sat on rickety benches at rough tables. Anya led the program with several young people helping. Our girls knew Anya and felt comfortable enough to join the group, even though they understood little.

Janelle and Alicia used the language of play to make friends. Janelle taught other little girls "Ring-Around-the-Rosy" and the alphabet song. Older children wanted to hold Alicia, but Alicia didn't want to be held.

Sometimes Anya took the girls to her apartment during our Russian lesson and kept them occupied with dolls and drawing supplies. Her cat went into hiding after Alicia attacked it.

Anya took me to the post office to buy stamps one day. The woman behind the counter seemed very angry. I didn't understand why it was such a big ordeal but was glad I had Anya nearby to reason with the woman. Not until later did I realize I had asked for two hundred stamps instead of twenty. She didn't have two hundred stamps.

When I wanted a hair cut, Anya took me to a beauty salon. I got a shampoo, haircut, and blow-dry for about $1.20—the same price as four rolls of toilet paper. Anya told me later the hairdressers thought I was deaf since she spoke on my behalf, and they saw us using our form of sign language.

Not long after we moved into our apartment, three Americans arrived in Feodosia to see us before attending a meeting elsewhere. They brought us a coffee maker and other things we requested. It felt like Christmas.

The next day was terrible. To start with Cory committed the unpardonable sin of drinking all the coffee from our new coffee maker. Then I decided to tackle the dreaded task of washing clothes in the tub since we were running out of underwear. I lost my balance and leaned on our wobbly bathroom sink, sending it crashing to the floor. While Cory tried to fix it, I began washing dishes, putting them on the drying rack in the cupboard over the kitchen sink. The drying rack fell on my head, showering me with silverware, cups, and plates.

Mid-afternoon, the three American men came over for conversation and apple crisp. One asked me what I liked best about Ukraine. At the moment I couldn't think of a single thing. I finally mumbled, "Some of the people we have met."

"Safe answer," Cory told me later. Right. If you are going to be good missionaries, you are supposed to like the people. After more thought, I decided it was true: our new friends were the best part—or else our new indoor toilet.

One of the men, Jim Penhollow, had been a missionary, so I asked him, "What advice would you as a veteran give to a beginner?"

"Don't feel like you have to do it all at once," he said.

I thought of his words many times in the coming months since I often felt overwhelmed by the demands of housework, language study, child care, and my desire to build relationships.

The playground near our apartment featured this "slideless" slide

Our apartment was upstairs from a grocery store

Many Russians visit Feodosia for the vacation

Painters sell their artwork by the gallery

- 5 -
Garlic and Pig Fat

Since Giorgi and his family helped us so much when we lived on the hill, we invited them to our new home for dinner. What should I fix? Not borscht. I could make flour tortillas—how about burritos?

A trip to the meat market was always a challenge. Using a long fork provided, I poked at mysterious mounds of flesh until something with a reasonable price looked good enough.

I boiled the bone and meat with beans and ran the whole mess—minus the bone—through our meat grinder. Juice dripped around the handle onto the floor. Needing sour cream, I trotted back to the market with a jar. In the dairy products building, women stood behind piles of curds and buckets of sour cream. A woman dabbed sour cream on my wrist for a taste. Good enough, so I gave her my jar to fill.

Giorgi and Luba brought three of their five children and a delicious cake. They removed their shoes at the door—like good Ukrainians—but since my floor wasn't clean, I wished they hadn't. Mopping, even sweeping, hadn't been high on my priority list. ("Don't feel like you have to do it all now," I kept telling myself.)

Luba started washing dishes immediately. She didn't let me help when we visited their home but pitched right in when visiting us. They seemed to like the burritos and fruit jello, at least they were polite enough to eat it.

Ukrainian housewives preserve produce in jars during the summer and fall for wintertime use. Wanting to learn how to can the Russian way, I visited Olga on one of her canning days. I helped her chop up eggplant, green peppers, and onions for some kind of vegetable relish.

I did not intend to copy her recipe, but I enjoyed the fellowship and wanted to learn from her. She ladled the boiling mixture into hot jars and sealed the lids with a tool that crimps the lids around the rim of the jars. The process was more difficult than the American method, but it worked.

I bought jars and lids at the market and borrowed a crimping tool from a neighbor. Though the summer fruit season had passed already, I found raspberries for jam and ingredients for salsa and pickle relish.

Cory brought variety to language studies by helping church members construct a Christian education wing. "I don't even care that much about the building itself," he told me, "I just see it as a good way to build relationships."

He hauled sand and rocks for cement while learning the Russian words for bucket, brick, and hurry up. He mixed cement by hand and dug trenches in the hard clay. Over lunch he learned about *salo*, slices of raw pig fat, served with bread and raw garlic cloves. He never developed a taste for salo but learned to like borscht.

Meal times helped Cory get to know people better and gave him opportunities to practice his Russian. One day, his fellow workers asked if we had bread in America.

"Of course," Cory said. He explained that big companies make it, and we buy it in stores.

"How does it stay fresh?" someone asked.

Since some Russian words are a variation of the English, Cory tried "preservatives" with a Russian accent. The table got very quiet. Apparently, he stumbled on a Russian word that had something to do with birth control.

Old women at the construction site had much advice for Cory. They told him not to work so hard. He should eat more. They rebuked him for whistling, since whistling brings poverty. He should carry bricks a certain way. They didn't want to fill his bucket completely with mortar so it wouldn't be too heavy.

Cory figured if we are going to work, let's work hard and get it done, and got impatient with the snail's pace. Some were surprised an American could do physical labor. One man said he had heard that Americans work hard and by watching Cory, he saw it was true.

Tatiana, our language helper, explained how socialism affected the work ethic. "We were told to work hard, but if someone produced more on the job, the expected quota was raised for all the workers in order to get the same salary. So the harder you worked, the less you got paid."

Cory got frequent comments on the white cotton socks he wore to work. Cotton is expensive in Ukraine and white socks were rare. He finally gave up trying to explain that those were his work socks and started wearing dark dress socks to the construction site.

Several families in the church invited us over for meals. These visits gave us opportunities to practice our Russian, build relationships, and learn more about the culture. When they pulled out the photo album after dinner, we saw that many in the church were related.

One family lived right across the courtyard from our apartment. The grandmother, Ludmila; her daughter, Gallia; and five-year-old Natasha lived together. Ludmila, the church matriarch, was usually the first one to pray after the first sermon and often recited a poem after the second sermon. Poetry and prayers in church gave women their opportunity to preach.

Gallia, age thirty-one, had long, beautiful blond hair. I saw her in makeup and jewelry on her way to work but never in church. Her husband lived in Siberia with his parents and worked in a flourmill where he made more money than he could in Crimea. He sent money occasionally, and they saw each other once or twice a year.

Gallia's apartment felt homey with carpet, curtains, and china cabinet. She served cabbage rolls stuffed with rice and hamburger, followed by cake and tea. I felt positively pampered.

When I took the girls to their apartment to play with Natasha another day, I saw what a typical meal was like. Grandma Ludmila fried potatoes for us. She served no meat, just slices of salo, the raw pork fat—with bread and eggplant relish. I skipped the salo.

Stefan and his wife, Nadia, also invited us to their home for dinner. They had four older children ranging in age from ten to fifteen plus a five-year-old daughter. The two older girls wanted to hold Alicia. Janelle ran around the apartment with the smallest girl and the younger boy. Cory swapped fish stories with Stefan.

Stefan lived in a newer housing development, about twenty minutes by foot from our place. His apartment building was very new, but parts of cement stairway had already crumbled away. There was no landscaping, just a mud-hole out front and a rusting building crane.

I was glad we lived in the center of town. Our apartment was smaller, but at least we had big trees around us. We also lived closer to the beach, the market, and parks with flowerbeds and functional benches.

Some time later, I invited Stefan's family over for dinner. Stefan had already helped us so much and this night was no exception. He brought scrap lumber and, after dinner, he made shelves for our small storage closet.

Nadia helped me wash dishes. The water had been off all afternoon, as usual, but fortunately I had saved some that morning. After going without a few times, I learned to keep water on hand.

She told me, "It's bad without water. America must be much better."

"America has problems too," I replied.

"At least you can get a job in America if you want to work. Stefan used to work at the optics factory, but it's been closed for almost two years."

Lena, a fairly new Christian in her early 20s, spoke English and lived in the apartment building next to us. Lena earned around $30 a month working in an oil refinery. Since she handled toxic substances, they gave her a bonus of a half-liter bottle of milk daily to offset the health hazards.

"I feel dizzy at work sometimes," she said, "but I'm glad I have a job that pays. Many people have not been paid for several months, and it's hard to find work."

Lena's best friend attended a Bible school in the U.S. The friend wrote that Americans ruin good pork fat (bacon) by cooking it! And then they throw the grease away!

Since Lena understood English, we could talk freely about our own cultural adjustments. "Its hard not knowing what to expect," Cory said. "We don't know what is appropriate, what the rules are to the game."

"It's the same way for the people of Ukraine," Lena replied. "They have never lived in a non-communist country before. Everything changes so quickly, they don't know what to expect either."

I asked her why the old women always cry when they pray in church. "Their lives are very difficult," she said. "The pensioners receive only $10 a month to live on."

The retired pastor of the Feodosia church, Ivan Mikalovich, also invited us for a meal. His name translates to: "John, son of Michael." Since he was an older man, worthy of respect, no one would say his first name without including "Mikalovich." One might call him "Mikalovich" alone but never just Ivan.

The old pastor had a kind face and the bushiest eyebrows I've ever seen. He was short and stocky. His short, round wife bustled from the kitchen to the sitting room bringing bowls of steaming borscht. Their never-married daughter, Tanya, lived with them and helped in the kitchen.

Everyone slurped cabbage soup from big spoons. "Toss out Emily Post," Cory murmured. Tanya served the second course: rice with tokens of meat and mashed potatoes with more meat garnish.

"You're so thin," Grandma said, drawing her fingers over her plump cheeks. "Is life in Ukraine hard for you? Your mother will be so worried when she sees you."

"Yes, it is difficult here, but this is normal," I assured her, touching my cheek.

We talked about our visit to the home of their son and grandchildren in Salem, Oregon. They missed those who emigrated. Grandma's eyes watered. It was too expensive to fly back and forth, but the emigrants called occasionally.

"How many children do you have?" I asked. Besides the son in Salem, they had seven other children. One served as a pastor in a village near Feodosia, four attended the Feodosia church and two sons hadn't accepted Christ.

When Ivan Mikalovich led the Feodosia church during Soviet times, he received threats and pressure from authorities. However, he had studied up on religious laws and procedures. When authorities told him, "You can't do that," he would say, "According to your handbook, I can." Then he'd refer to the section and paragraph. Under his leadership, the Feodosia church planted three churches in the surrounding region.

Tanya served the third course: apple cake and apple-raspberry juice. Grandma sent us home with leftover cake plus jars of relish, jam, and juice. Their warm hospitality brought tears to my eyes.

Most of all we wanted to build a good relationship with the current pastor, Igor, and his wife Olga. They invited us over for dinner and came to our home as well. We learned that Igor had moved to Feodosia at age seventeen and apprenticed as a shoe cobbler. He met Olga at the church and they married after his required two-year service in the military. Igor attended a Bible college in St. Petersburg, Russia and then became pastor of the Feodosia church. He had served in this role for three years.

Igor stopped at our house one day to confide in Cory. He was frustrated that others in the church, especially the men, didn't help enough with the building project. "You see how hard I work," he said. "Why don't they have the same commitment? If we all work hard for a few months, then we'll be done. It's difficult to forgive them and be open to them. Maybe they don't respect me because of my age." He was thirty-five, younger than most on the church council.

Cory just listened.

"Do American churches have this problem too…people lacking commitment?"

"Yes, we have the same problem. Pastors can be very lonely. Even though they are surrounded by many people, few in the congregation really understand them. I want you to know that I pray for you every day. Can we pray together now?"

They did. Cory suggested they meet regularly to talk and pray.

"That's a good idea," Igor said, "maybe at the church, before work."

When Igor left, Cory told me about the conversation. "This will be a good way to get to know him better and build our relationship. He's always been so distant before. Igor has such a strong personality. Even when I didn't know much Russian I could see it at the worksite. He criticizes people so much I understand why they don't like working with him. Still, he's lonely and I want to support him."

Several days later, Cory returned from the church and said, "I still haven't met with Igor again. He told me today he feels too overwhelmed by all he needs to do and it's just one more thing. I guess I'll just keep making myself available."

- 6 -
Garage Sale Paradise

Those first months when entering the market, I'd take a deep breath as though bracing myself for a cold shower. I disliked the noise, the confusion. Would I understand when they told me the price? Would I find the right change? Should I buy small dirty carrots for less or pay more for big ones? Was I extravagant to buy cheese and butter?

I missed the convenience of shopping in America. I missed shopping carts, well-stocked aisles, and clearly marked prices. I missed parking lots and cars with trunks. At least the market was only a five-minute walk from our new apartment.

Several women warned me I should stock up on food and produce for the winter, so I took the challenge seriously. I bought about eighty pounds of potatoes, carrying them home in two trips on my luggage cart. I bought onions, carrots, apples, flour, sugar, and beans.

I'd seen other people shopping with something like a luggage cart. I tried to use ours, but it gave me one more thing to haul up four flights of stairs. Besides, I never got the knack of stacking it properly. After I spilled rice all over the sidewalk, I left the cart at home and joined the ranks of those who carried plastic shopping bags everywhere.

Once I got my serious shopping done for winter and didn't have to haul so much, I enjoyed my trips to the market more. I learned to go early, so I wouldn't have to fight the crowds. Folk music or the songs of a Russian rock star blared over the loudspeaker where cassette tapes sold. I could smell meat-filled pastries frying.

In the clothing section, vendors stood on tables in their booths hanging up sweaters, jeans, and sweat pants. In open areas, women lined up holding coats, shoes, and other clothing for sale. I walked down the row of booths where they sold ketchup and mayonnaise from Poland, dates from Turkey, macaroni, and open boxes of bulk cookies. I saw interesting brand names. I found "Sunny" tape recorders and "Seeko" clocks. I saw "Rebook" clothes and "Gross" shampoo.

In the covered produce section, I continued my search for good apple-sauce apples, then wandered around back to look at the winter boots. It was a "one-stop-shopping" market.

At the "garage sale" section of the market, elderly women sold old clothes, books, buttons, and silverware. One old woman offered a crystal bowl for $3. I bought a Russian village scene carved in wood for $1.20 from a grateful woman; perhaps she needed potato money for the winter. I found a flour sifter and went home to get the bugs out of my flour.

Apple juice came in three-liter jars. These jars made good storage containers for staples like flour, sugar, beans, and rice. They kept the bugs out, or at least confined.

I was excited to find raisins at the market one day and bought two kilograms. While making bread pudding, I discovered worms in my prize raisins. I washed the worms and worm droppings out of my raisins and re-dried them in the oven.

I soon visited every store downtown looking for things to make our apartment more comfortable. Shopping in Ukraine was the ultimate garage-sale fanatic's paradise. Like garage sales, selection was limited and I never knew what I'd find. I saw pillows at the bookstore, dresses at the food store, and pickles in the clothing store. A hardware store had one pair of thick soled shoes—good luck trying to find your size.

The demands of living cut back on time available for language study, but my outings gave me opportunities to practice Russian. When buying bread one day at a kiosk near our apartment, I wanted a loaf of the yellow sweet bread. The woman looked puzzled, so I pointed out what I wanted. I later realized I had asked for "green" bread.

Bread is the most important part of a Ukrainian/Russian meal. Some bread lines in Soviet history were caused by scarcity, but the bread lines I saw were because bread is purchased daily. Give us this day our daily bread. Most families eat bread without anything on it, except as dessert, when it's served with thick slices of butter.

When I learned how to say, "Is this bread fresh?" I could understand all conversation in the bread store. The options available lay on a high shelf with the price listed, while racks and racks of bare loaves waited behind the counter. The heavy, brown loaf was 36 thousand; sour white bread was 44 thousand; fluffy white for 56 thousand; plus some rolls, a big bran bun, and a long white loaf.

The first woman in line might say, "Is 44 fresh?"

"No."

"Which is fresh?"

Some people wanted only half a loaf, so the cashier cut a chunk in two. While her back was turned, customers squeezed the half-loaves on the counter testing for freshness.

I continued to buy milk from the milk truck. When there wasn't a line, I talked with the woman who dipped milk from a big kettle and the man who took the money.

"Where are you from?" she asked one day.

"I'm American."

She looked surprised. Many Ukrainians sought to emigrate to the U.S., so people found it hard to believe an American wanted to live in Ukraine.

"Where is it better, America or Ukraine?" she asked. It was a common question.

"They are just different," I replied. "America is America. Ukraine is Ukraine."

One day there was a long line at the milk truck. As much as I hate to stand in line for anything, I also hate paying more than necessary. I figured that if I didn't get in line, I would have to buy milk from the store for double the price. I got in line like a good Russian but wondered what the holdup was.

Suddenly, the herd started to stampede, crowding toward the truck. I didn't have enough Russian to ask what was going on. It appeared they were about out of milk and everyone panicked. The woman dispensing milk kept motioning for me to give her my bottle. I finally did when it was almost my turn. Two old ladies argued as to who was next in line behind me and several others begged for some of my milk, like a pack of dogs fighting over a few morsels. I escaped with my full jar of milk but wondered what I should have done differently. I felt bad later, certain those old women needed the cheap milk more than I did.

This milk came from collective farms where they removed most of the cream for butter. Many housewives disdained this low-fat product from hundreds of anonymous cows and careless workers. The milk did taste strange occasionally.

The last time I bought milk from the truck, I took it home to cook it, as usual. I noticed the skin that formed on top was a little brown, as if it had chocolate added...or mud...or...well, I tried not to about think what else it might be. When I saw sludge at the bottom, I dumped it down the drain.

After that, I decided it's not too hard to buy milk at the market. Sure, I had to face the mob of women in the milk building all inviting me to taste their milk, but there was better quality control.

If something doesn't fit, could I take it back? I knew how shops operated in the U.S. but felt uncertain in Ukraine. With cooler weather, I bought some thick, black stockings at the market. At home, I discovered the waist-length stockings wouldn't pull up much past my knees. Now what?

I looked up "it doesn't fit" in my Russian-English phrase book, went back to the market and forgot how to say it. Nevertheless, the woman understood and pulled out the refund. I felt sorry she lost her sale, so I bought a "Seeko" clock from her, made in China.

On a side street near the market was an outdoor hardware "store." Old men sold car parts, plumbing supplies, wire, and tools—all set out on sheets of plastic on the ground. It was the best place to go for all your hardware needs.

Not far from there, I found young animals for sale. Janelle and Alicia liked to visit this "petting zoo." They inspected the chickens, baby ducks, goats, baby pigs, puppies, and rabbits.

Since our landlord didn't allow a cat or dog, we got a parakeet. We bought a young bird at the market for $3 plus a hand-made cage, feeder, and food for another $3. The girls were excited about the new addition to the family and decided to call him "Malinki" which is "little" in Russian. They heard "malinki" often from people talking about the "little" girls.

As time went on, I got to know our neighbors. When water overflowed in the kitchen, our neighbor from downstairs knocked on the door. Our water pressure was so low, I had left the faucet on to fill a pot, then got distracted.

"I have water dripping into my apartment," she complained.

I bought her flowers. It appeased her until a pipe to our toilet started to drip.

A widow living two floors below us often sat at her balcony window and watched the world go by. When she saw me coming home or heard the girls rattling up or down the stairs, she opened her door for a chat.

The first time I talked with her, she cried through much of our visit. She showed me the photo of her husband who died a year earlier.

"I'm all alone," she said. "My daughter lives in Sevastopol."

She was too crippled to walk as far as the market, so I gave her produce occasionally. She cried every time. Perhaps she wasn't used to kindness from people. Since she cried so much, I referred to her as "the weeping widow."

She told me she was eighty years old. I commented she had seen much. She nodded and cried some more. She made the motion of her hands being tied together, said something about war, and talked about her operations. I wished I could understand more Russian.

Our stairwell had four doors on each landing. One door on our landing belonged to a young mother, Katya, who lived with her husband and their one-and-a-half-year-old daughter. She had long, bleached-blond hair with a wide row of black roots showing—platinum blond was in fashion then—and she wore skinny black leggings with platform shoes. One day she invited me to come visit sometime.

I wasn't sure when I should go, since she never suggested a day, but after several more vague invitations, I baked an applesauce cake and took it over.

She invited me in and motioned towards a bed-couch in her simple one-room apartment. Though her street clothes indicated she had money, her apartment told a different story. I sat on wet blankets, which smelled of urine. It's not "Russian" to use diapers, although I'd seen expensive, imported disposables at the market. Russian children more typically go through many changes of clothing.

I thought Janelle and Alicia would like to play with her little girl, but they stood glued to a old television set that dominated the small room. The husband came home from work and scrambled to find something to serve the American guests. He opened a jar of fruit juice for the girls and asked if I would like a cognac.

"No thank you," I said, hoping he wouldn't be offended.

He asked many questions about who we were and what we were doing there. I told them Cory was at the church helping them build.

"He pays for the building?" he said, rubbing his thumb against his fingers.

"Nyet," I said, and made motions of shoveling. He seemed surprised an American would do such work.

I came home and thought how contentment depends on with whom you compare yourself. Our apartment was shabby and small by American standards, but a palace compared to our neighbors' place.

The woman living on the other side of our wall gave us a warm welcome when we first moved in and was a great neighbor. Since we could hear her cough, hear her snore, and hear her television, I'm sure she got an earful from our side of the wall. When I asked her if the girls were too loud, however, she shook her head and said with a kindly smile, "Oh no, children will be children."

Our favorite neighbor was Anya, and we saw her almost every day. Since she worked at the post office, she brought us our mail. She frequently brought ice cream bars or candy for the girls, too. I wished she wouldn't spend her precious, hard-earned money on us.

Anya often took the girls for a walk to the Black Sea where they liked to throw rocks in the water. Sometimes I'd go with them. In spite of the language barrier, we could understand each other pretty well.

As Cory's birthday approached, she said she wanted to help celebrate and said something about dinner. I baked a cake and looked forward to a relaxing evening at her house. On our way over, we met Anya and Lena, carrying flowers and candy, coming to our house for dinner! Whoops.

Fortunately, I had hamburger in the fridge. Thirty-five minutes later, we sat down to rice and hamburger gravy. At least I didn't have to kill the fatted calf. We had a surprise birthday party for Cory. The surprise was learning I was the hostess.

Cabbage is an important part of the Ukrainian diet

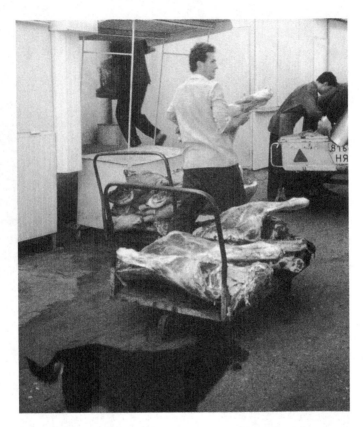

Surprisingly, stray dogs left meat at the market alone

- 7 -
Off the Pedestal

Those who think missionaries are "super saints" probably don't know any very well. Our new roles brought new kinds of stress, which like a refiner's fire, brought impurities to the surface. We didn't always cope very well.

Cory and I both had to learn the language, so we tried to find ways to divide household tasks. He helped wash dishes and clothes; he packed out the trash and tutored Janelle in preschool games on the computer.

I appreciated his help (at least sometimes I did) but laughed when I saw a Beetle Bailey comic strip at our teammate's house in Melitopol. The general's wife declared, "If you are going to retire soon, you will have to help around the house." No problem, he said—but whatever he did, he didn't do it the way she would.

It's not that men are inept or anything, it's just that they're in trouble if they don't help and in trouble if they do. It was good for both of us that Cory went down to the church occasionally to throw bricks around and do the male bonding thing.

Cory's reluctance to help with shopping made me upset. He never liked shopping in the U.S. and felt even more overwhelmed in Ukraine. I was more familiar with outdoor markets from my time in Kenya but I still thought, *Why should I have to pack it all home?*

When he had bought furniture, he felt nervous spending a lot of money, not wanting to attract attention. Igor, who helped him, had his car broken into often afterwards. Cory had seen someone watching him and following him when he went out, so he shaved his mustache in order to change his appearance.

We had heard tales of mafia crime. The previous summer, mafia hit men killed several Tatar businessmen in Feodosia. The Tatar rose up and destroyed a mafia-owned restaurant. More Tatar died in retaliation attacks. The summer before that, an apartment above Anya's was bombed after a businessman didn't pay his tax to the mafia.

Several weeks after we moved into our apartment, we heard a gunshot outside. We looked out and saw a man lying in a pool of blood. We learned later, it was a mafia hit. Presumably, someone didn't pay up when threatened. This incident heightened Cory's sense of concern

Still, I resented having to pack everything home from the market. One day I asked him to buy me some bread, and then went for a walk with Anya and the girls. When I came home, Cory emerged from the bedroom with eyes red and puffy.

"I'm sorry," he said. "I didn't get any bread. I can't. I don't know why. I just can't. I'm ready to go home. I'm not cut out to be a missionary."

When a couple heads to the mission field, it's like jumping into the deep end of a swimming pool when you don't know how to swim. It's hard to offer much support to your spouse while thrashing around trying to keep yourself from going under. Someone advised us before we moved to Ukraine, "Give each other the freedom to struggle."

We got a newsletter from friends who were also new missionaries. In the midst of phrases describing the new sights, sounds, and feelings were the words, "What happened to the person I married?"

I wondered what happened to the strong, fun-loving man I once knew. Cory probably wondered what happened to his affectionate, easy-going wife.

Later he came to the conviction he could not let fear rule him, and he became a more confident shopper. Nevertheless, I let each additional transgression build on and reinforce that firmly placed cornerstone, his failure to help me in the beginning like I wanted. I focused on his faults so much I didn't see my own. His acts of kindness and words of affirmation bounced off my shell.

I came to understand why a missionary couple I knew ended up getting a divorce. I could see why our mission organization required recruits to meet with a counselor before acceptance. Eventually, I found the freedom that results from forgiving your spouse for not being God.

I was better suited anyway for shopping in a "hunting and gathering society" like Ukraine. I was a garage sale shopper even in the U.S. As head cook, I knew what would enhance our menu. If I sent my husband out to buy eggs, it would never occur to him to buy raisins.

Though I had to cope with housework, in some ways it was easier than Cory's job. I knew how to cook and clean, but he had to figure out how to minister in a different culture.

He came home barking occasionally, and I'd bark back. "I don't like it when you take out your frustrations on us," I said once.

He looked at me soberly and asked, "Who else can I vent with?" Neither of us had the outside supports we once enjoyed.

Some days, I woke up growling. I felt more angry, more often than I had in my whole life. I disliked the inconveniences, the sense of isolation, the language barrier, the hard work. I wondered, *will I ever feel at home?* Family, especially Cory, got the brunt of it. I wrote in my journal:

Some people believe in purgatory, the idea of getting cleaned up for heaven after death. I think God uses life to get us ready for Glory, to burn up the chaff so we can look and act like Jesus. I want to shine like gold, but I don't like the fire.

I used to think of God's calling as a place or profession. Now I see He isn't as concerned about the good we do for Him, as much as the good He can put in us. Obeying His call to a place or profession is a good way to prepare for corrective surgery.

We came to Ukraine in hopes of a fruitful harvest. Paul talked about being poured-out wine for the sake of others. Grapes must be crushed to make wine. Sour grapes don't make sweet wine, so God is perfecting the fruit in me.

When I prayed with the girls at the end of the day, I tried to think of things for which we could be thankful. In my depressed state, my list was often pretty basic. "Thank you that we have beds to sleep in and food to eat. And I pray for the people who don't know Jesus."

The girls often prayed for "the people who don't know Jesus." Alicia lengthened her usual prayer to include "...the people who don't have food...the people who don't have legs...the people who don't have binkies." Alicia, at age two, was still quite attached to her pacifier.

Early in October, we found and bought a Russian washing machine. Though still labor intensive, it was a great improvement after washing clothes by hand for two months. It had two sections: one side for washing and the other side for spinning out the water.

We tried it out immediately. First step: pour water into the wash side. Since we didn't have running hot water, I heated some on the stove. I learned not to put too many clothes in the water; otherwise, they wound up in knots and didn't get clean.

After several minutes of churning, I transferred the clothes into the centrifuge chamber. The water from the "spin dry" side pumped back into the wash side. I rinsed the clothes in the tub and spun them out again. The washing machine was small enough to store under the coat rack in our entryway.

During one washday, Alicia gave her plastic cat and *The Jungle Book* cassette a bath. Cory took the tape apart to dry. Alicia discovered the tape on a windowsill and had to inspect its innards.

A frustrated mother gathered small pieces together and struggled to rewind the sprawling tape. Alicia tried to crawl on my lap but I pushed her away. With her attempt at reconciliation ignored, Alicia burst into song, "He's still working on me."

Janelle asked, "Is He still working on you too, Mommy?"

One day Anya came over to warn us that the water would be turned off the next morning for three days for the biannual cleaning of the system. I spent the rest of the day filling every container I could find with water.

Pots of water covered my stove. Jars and bowls of water hid the small kitchen counter. Most of the kitchen floor was covered with full laundry tubs, jars, and jugs. I washed out the bathroom tub and filled it with water too. By the next morning, the tub water had leaked out, but I still had plenty to last for our three-day drought.

Two weeks later, Anya came to tell us the water would go off again for one day, so they could add chlorine to the system. I tried to gather water but found it was already off.

Anya got water again when expected but we didn't. Our building had a broken water pipe, and we went without running water for several days. Cory hauled buckets up to our fourth-floor apartment from Anya's.

Grandma Ludmila, a believer living across the courtyard, invited us to bathe at her place. She put the girls in the tub and filled it with water chest-deep. "That's enough! That's enough!" Janelle cried. Next Grandma soaped them down good and proper with a rough scrubbing cloth and put them through the rinse cycle before she let them get out.

Fortunately, she let me shower alone.

It took discipline to squeeze much language study into a day filled with shopping, cooking, cleaning, water storage, and childcare. Many missionaries—especially in developing countries—make use of household help. In many countries, it's expected. It didn't seem appropriate for us, though. Years of Soviet rule taught that everyone should be equal, and the virtuous work hard. Those with servants in pre-socialist days were thought of as evil oppressors.

Besides, I wasn't ready to give up my kitchen. I felt inept at many things, but at least I could cook and needed something in my routine I liked to do. I wasn't so fond of cleaning but knew it would drive me crazy to have another woman cleaning my house. Perhaps I got an extra dose of independence or have an overactive desire to do things my way.

We received a three-month visa when we came to Ukraine and approached the time for visa renewal with foreboding. In some ways, we hoped our application would be denied—at least then we could go home and save face. Life in Ukraine was more difficult than we expected.

On the other hand, I wasn't quite ready to pack my bags. After all, I had eighty pounds of potatoes stored on the balcony for winter use. Also I found pleasure in the small victories: understanding someone and being understood, successfully purchasing ten stamps at the post office all by myself, finding freshly baked bread, still warm.

Igor took Cory to Simferopol, two hours away, to renew our visa. Officials yelled at them for not having the proper documents. They visited several offices for signatures and stamps of approval and had to make a second trip to the capitol city before we finally got a visa for three more months. Cory found the whole process very stressful.

"This place wasn't designed for people but for robots," he grumbled when he got home. "These bureaucrats have so many rules and change them without telling anyone. If you don't do everything right, you're in trouble. The whole system is based on control. I understand why people get drunk. I hate it here. I want to go home."

I just listened and served him dinner. He'd get over it.

The need to renew our visa every three months kept us on edge and made it more difficult to put down roots. We didn't want to make major purchases for the apartment, like a big refrigerator or new linoleum, only to get kicked out of the country soon afterwards.

Though we may have wanted the easy out—getting expelled from the country—God had other plans for us.

Cory built relationships while helping church members with construction

- 8 -
Walking in the Dark

We lived in Ukraine, so I assumed the people were "Ukrainians." Many corrected me however, "I am not Ukrainian. I am Russian." Though Crimea is part of Ukraine, most people there, especially in larger cities, are ethnically Russian, not Ukrainian.

I heard you could tell a Ukrainian town is pro-Russia if they still had their statue of Lenin standing. Feodosia's giant-sized Lenin kept his prominent place in a large square in front of the train station. Our mayor and most of the city council were Communist.

During Soviet times, November 7 was a national holiday celebrating the Socialist Revolution. Western Ukraine stopped honoring this day, but Crimea continued to observe this communist holiday.

I took the girls for a walk in the rain that day, following the sound of a band playing. We came upon a large gathering in front of the train station. People wearing dark overcoats and carrying umbrellas laid flowers at the feet of "Father" Lenin's thirty-foot statue. The band played another piece and marched down the road. Men in uniform followed the band, carrying red flags with the hammer and sickle symbol. Others carried communist slogans and the herd of umbrellas moved to another park.

I watched a woman rearrange the flowers then followed the parade. Around two or three hundred people gathered; most were elderly. After a brief speech, the band played again.

Janelle, whose only experience with band music was a funeral procession, asked, "Did somebody die?" *More than we'll ever know, my little one.*

During Soviet times, the city provided hot water and heat to all apartment buildings. Feodosia's apartments hadn't had heat for three years.

I wrote in my journal, November 8:

> It still hasn't frosted here, but wind and rain have stripped most leaves from the trees outside. Our thermometer inside says it's 14 degrees Centigrade in the house, whatever that means. It means I'm sitting here in two shirts, a sweater, and long underwear. My feet are tucked under a pot of stewed chicken to keep them warm. I figured I might as well use that heat for something useful. Our electric heater gives out enough to keep off the chill. At least we can afford the electricity, which makes it easier for us than for most.

I had paid for the month's allotment of cooking gas. A couple of weeks later, it finally came on but lasted a scant two weeks. Not all residents had been able to pay, and many used their kitchen stoves as heaters.

Mid-November, our radiators felt slightly warm when we touched them. I finally found a conversion chart for Centigrade. When the radiators were on, the living area stayed a comfy 14 degrees—or 57 degrees Fahrenheit. Our kitchen and bathroom side of the house was 52 degrees, unless I did much cooking. With our electric heater on full blast, our living room got up to 61, maybe even 62. We lived in our long underwear.

Power outages began in earnest mid-November. Many people had not paid their electric bill and the state could not afford to give away free electricity. The state couldn't afford to pay salaries either, so people didn't have money to pay their bills.

Our electricity typically went out twice a day, morning and evening, for two hours—four hours total. It wasn't so bad during the day, but it made for long evenings. The outages often followed a regular schedule but not always.

One morning, the electricity was off and the gas to our stove quit before I could make breakfast. I served bread and applesauce, since cold cereal wasn't available.

Janelle interrupted Cory's breakfast prayer, "Daddy, Daddy, we don't have to pray because our food isn't hot." Prayer is something you do while waiting for your food to cool.

The electricity went off again that afternoon. I didn't know what to do for dinner with no gas and no electricity, then the phone rang. Lena offered to bring us some food. She had made a tasty rice dish with carrots and onions and chicken before the electricity went out. It glistened with grease in the flickering candlelight. I asked her how she made it.

"You put a cup of oil in the pan," she said first, then listed the other ingredients. Russians eat high-fat diets to help them keep warm. Maybe I should have done likewise, since I felt cold all winter.

Few public buildings were heated, including schools and hospitals. Children sat in classrooms so cold they could see their breath. Despite heavy clothing, it's hard to concentrate with numb feet and hard to write when wearing mittens.

When Stefan's daughter had pneumonia, they took her to the hospital. The hospital was unheated, had no medicines, and served only one meal a day. They decided she'd be better off at home.

Though our apartment was cold, Anya and Lena always said how warm it felt. They couldn't afford electricity, so they used no heat. Our neighbor answered her door wearing a heavy coat. At the market, old women sat in the cold trying to sell sunflower seeds or homemade socks to earn bread money. My life was easy compared to many, so I felt I couldn't, or shouldn't, complain.

People talked about the good old days, when buildings had heat and workers got paid. Nevertheless I learned people suffered during Soviet times too. In Stalin's day, authorities confiscated almost all their food. While grain was sold for export, many died from starvation.

Tatiana ate dinner with us after her work and before our Russian lesson. When I served cornbread one evening, she told us of a time when she was a girl and the only bread available was horrible cornbread.

Even when the Greeks ruled, Crimea was known as a wheat-producing region. Then President Khrushchev visited United States and saw miles and miles of cornfields in the Midwest. When he returned home, he had all the wheat fields plowed under and planted into corn.

Tatiana said they could get wheat bread only by a doctor's prescription. She remembered standing in line for six hours as a child to buy macaroni, typically a staple in Crimea. Each person in line could buy only one kilogram.

Though food shortages are uncommon now, prices are higher and life is difficult. Most factories have closed. People can't find work and women can't feed their families as well as they once did.

Tatiana said a colleague at work had a husband who was a retired rocket scientist. He once made a good salary but received a very small pension so they lived off what the wife made at the art gallery. She could no longer afford to buy meat or even bones for broth, so she made her borscht very thick, hoping he wouldn't notice.

He still hadn't noticed. Every time he ate her borscht he would say, "You must be more careful. I found another small bone today." She could not tell him the truth.

One day while the girls napped and Cory was gone, the doorbell rang. A poorly dressed woman stood outside without coat or hat. "Please," she said, "give me some money for food for my children." I invited her in and gave her milk and eggs. She asked for sugar. I wanted to send her to someone from the church that spoke better Russian—let her be someone else's problem—but I gave her sugar. She asked for butter, then soap, then money for bread. I gave her margarine, soap, about $1.00 and a jar of salted cabbage someone gave us. She asked for a coat and boots.

I'm sure she needed them, but I started to feel irritated. I'm not a Salvation Army distributor. I gave her a Gospel tract in Russian, hoping it would give her a different kind of help. She left with many thanks. I thought afterwards, maybe I should have done more. I prayed God would touch her life in ways I couldn't.

Two days later, another woman rang our doorbell and asked for food or financial help. I shook my head and closed the door. Mother Theresa wouldn't have done that. I felt guilty, but I didn't want the whole city to start lining up outside our apartment.

After talking with others, I settled on a policy of giving away a few apples or some bread when someone came begging at our door.

Church services were held Saturday night, Sunday morning, and Sunday night. Every service lasted two hours, with three sermons. Cory tried to attend each one as a way to learn Russian, build relationships, and show his support of the church. I figured Sunday morning was enough for the girls and me.

When cold weather hit, the girls stayed home, especially when Janelle was sick. I couldn't expect them to sit through a two-hour service when it was cold enough to see our breath inside. When they couldn't go, Cory stayed home and held Sunday School for them while I went to the morning meeting.

I layered on two sweaters, wore long johns and stretch pants under my long skirt, added a coat, boots, and hat and headed off to church with Anya. No one lingered outside to talk; everyone sat bundled up in hats, scarves, and coats. In spite of my many layers, my toes grew numb before the service ended. An unheated church building does eliminate the need for a coat rack.

By mid-December, church construction had progressed enough so the radiator worked. I still wore many layers for the cold walk, but I could sit through the service without my toes turning to ice.

We had an English/Russian parallel Bible, which made it easier to follow along. I noticed First Peter was a favorite book for many sermons. With his many references to suffering, it seemed Peter could have been talking to the Russian church. After moving to Feodosia, I saw the Bible had much to say about suffering—things I hadn't noticed before.

They served communion on the first Sunday of the month. The deacons passed around plates with pieces of bread to the standing members. Then they brought a single cup around. Though the church condemned drunkenness, they used real wine for communion. As I listened to sick people cough, I hoped there was enough alcohol in it to kill the germs.

Cory sat through many candlelit services on Saturday and Sunday evenings when the electricity was off. Walking home without streetlights, he reflected on how our time in Ukraine was like walking in the dark.

"We barely know the language," he told me when he got home. "We don't know what's appropriate. We don't know when we are offending someone. We came with ideas of how we would like to help, but we are only beginning to see how complex the problems are and how much we really don't know." We needed Jesus to light our path.

E-mail was usually a great encouragement. We got many supportive notes from people who said they were praying for us. One note struck me the wrong way, however.

The woman had read our newsletter, which summarized our first four months in Ukraine. She said some missionaries get so focused on hardships that it overshadows their work, and she hoped we would get settled in soon and get on with the task at hand. She told of different people from her church who had gone on wonderful short-term trips to Ukraine.

She probably meant well, but that note pushed some buttons. If we had been in a language school somewhere, no one would have expected any reports on the number of conversions. We wanted to learn the language and culture at the same time, and we were glad we didn't have to offer a bunch of answers until we understood the questions.

Cory declined invitations to preach. "Not yet," he said. After all, Jesus was in His host country about thirty years before He gave a sermon. One year wasn't too long to wait and learn.

We didn't want to plant just one church or see a few people accept Christ; we wanted to help start a church planting movement. We wanted to train leaders who would plant churches and train others to plant more churches. We needed time and a solid foundation in order to reach that goal.

Long-term effectiveness needs more than a few quick and easy answers. Two months earlier, we had attended a concert put on by three American Christians visiting Feodosia. Between songs, they took turns telling how they tried different things looking for happiness and finally tried Jesus. One girl said she tried acting and wasn't happy so she tried Jesus, and she has been happy every single moment since.

I heard that 250 young people went forward that night. Such numbers make exciting reports back in the USA, but I wondered about the follow-up on those 250 people longing for happiness. Who would disciple them? When they hit rough spots, would they say they tried Christianity and it didn't work for them?

After four months we couldn't report 250 conversions, but seed scattered on shallow soil rarely takes root. Someone must plow and tend the crop. We planned to host short-term teams, but we hoped we could facilitate long-term results.

Besides learning the language, we wanted to understand the culture of Ukraine and our host church. Cory still hadn't been able to talk much with Igor.

"I'd like to get to know him and know what he thinks," Cory told me. "I want to ask him questions like: What does he believe is the purpose of the Church? How can it reach others for Christ? What should his focus be as a pastor? I want to ask him, how do you know if a person is really saved; is it by the head covering and lack of make-up?"

Cory got his chance when Igor took him to Simferopol to get some boxes that had come for us. The two-hour journey gave Cory time to ask many questions about the church and Igor's perspective on outreach.

Igor said his supervisor thought American churches were too liberal since they allow makeup and jewelry, and women don't wear head coverings. Christian women show true spirituality by humble appearance.

Cory pointed to a group of people waiting for the bus and asked, "How is the church going to reach them?" All those women wore makeup.

"I must get out and evangelize more," Igor replied.

"And when new people come to church, will they feel comfortable enough to stay?"

"They will change." Igor gave Anya as an example. We knew she wore makeup and jewelry to work, but she stopped wearing it to church after many rebukes.

Older believers, who hung on to their faith through years of persecution, said, "Why should we try to look like the world? We are supposed to be separate."

American Christians, who expect sixty minutes of "entertainment," have something to learn from the Russian church, which believes the presentation of truth has its own appeal. But perhaps the Russian church, which met in secret for seventy years for believers only, could learn something about opening their doors a little wider.

Igor said he recognized the need to reach out, but he felt pressure to honor church traditions. While they drove and talked, he got irritated occasionally.

Cory said, "It's my job to ask questions." He came home with a headache.

We got visitors from Kherson, a city in Ukraine where an American church helped start a new and growing congregation. The two men, an American and a Ukrainian, were traveling to another town in Crimea to look into the possibility of an American church partnering there.

They gave us additional insight on attitudes in the local church. The head of Baptist churches in Crimea was very opposed to American involvement, saying Americans are too liberal. Americans in Kherson and Simferopol had helped start new churches where women wore makeup and no head coverings.

The Russian Baptists believe that works don't save, but one shows faith by works. We heard of a woman who wanted to become a Christian, but the church wouldn't let her repent until she put on a head covering. Some churches kept a stack of headscarves to give to women who came unprepared.

In the old days, church members carefully submitted to church authorities so they wouldn't be excommunicated and have no place for Christian fellowship. Some leaders felt threatened by new churches, with their alternative place to worship.

We learned that church leaders in Crimea got together once to discuss the "problem" of American missionaries. Andre, a regional supervisor living in Feodosia, stood up and said, "People need to hear the Gospel. If we aren't doing the job, who are we to say that God can't send Americans to help us?"

It looked like an uphill battle, but we still wanted to work with the existing church. We didn't want to start from scratch and didn't want to start an American church. We didn't want a program so dependent on us it would die if we left the country.

Conversations gave us insight into how people viewed the church. Cory asked Anya why the church had so few men. She said men typically thought religion was for weak old women who cried a lot. Most men chose to drown their problems in alcohol instead.

Lena told us how hard it was to share her faith at work. At age twenty, she was one of the youngest workers at the oil refinery and got the job because she knew English. When she talked about her faith, other workers told her, "You are just a child and don't know about life." Some said they didn't want to become like her because then they couldn't steal and couldn't afford to live. Most employees took gas home to sell on the side.

Some told her, "If you want to go to church, you should go to the church of our parents, the Orthodox church." Any other church was called a sect.

I understood the term "sect" to the Russian is like "cult" to an American. Tatiana told us she was very surprised to learn the Russian Baptist Church was simply Protestant, similar to Protestant churches in Europe and the USA. She had always heard the Baptists were a small sect of foolish, misguided people. According to widespread propaganda, the Baptists had orgies and ate children.

She used to go to the Orthodox church to light candles for her mother when she had cancer but rarely went after her mom died. She explained that Orthodox believers rarely prayed directly to God, except for the rote prayers they learned. When they prayed from the heart, she said, they prayed to the saints or Mother Mary. They viewed God as unapproachable and hoped the saints would intercede on their behalf.

Each day of the year was assigned to a different saint. Tatiana, for example, was born on St. Tatiana's day, so she received that name. People prayed to the saint for whom they were named.

Feodosia had several Orthodox churches. While passing the largest one day, I stopped in for a closer look. I entered the courtyard and followed an old woman up to the cathedral's open doors. She paused, crossed herself, and went inside.

I stepped into an ornate room and saw many gold-framed paintings—icons featuring saints with halos, Madonna and child with halos, and Jesus with a halo. I gazed at the artwork on the vaulted ceiling. The room had no chairs because the Orthodox believe it is irreverent to sit in God's presence. A small booth at the entrance sold candles, crosses, icons, and booklets.

The woman who entered before me stopped in the center of the room and crossed herself in front of an ornate Madonna and child. She bowed with her forehead to the floor, got up, crossed herself again, and lit a small candle from a larger one burning there. She placed her candle in one opening of an ornate candleholder, and then repeated her acts of worship in front of other icons. Two other old women worshiped in similar fashion. One knelt in front of the image of Jesus on the cross, kissed his feet, and kissed the painted feet of weeping women at each side.

I stood and watched. The pictures were beautiful—the actions seemed strange. I wondered if these acts of worship brought them closer to God and made them more like Jesus.

Our method of worship probably also looks strange to the uninitiated. I know that whatever method is used, going through the motions doesn't change the heart.

Lena told us she used to sing in the Orthodox church choir before she became a Christian. She said the music, the service, and the building were beautiful, but she never heard the Gospel there.

When Lena attended the Baptist church, she learned she could have forgiveness of sins. She felt such joy inside after she gave her life to Christ. "I can't understand though, why the worship service in the Baptist church is so dreary," she said. "People tell me, 'Joy is something in your heart, not on your face.' Still, I think that joy in your heart should show on your face. I know solemn worship isn't wrong, but I don't want people to condemn me for showing joy."

We had more questions and fewer answers as time went on. How was the church to have any impact on society? How were we to have any impact when the church seemed set in its ways, and leaders were suspicious of American influence?

An Orthodox church in Ukraine

Icon corner in a home

-9-
Rat Hats and Cough Syrup

Cold wind blew through the cracks around our window frames. Mid-December, I finally stuffed paper in the openings to block out some of the wind. A few weeks later, I learned another winter weatherizing tip: cut strips of paper about two inches wide. Get one side wet and soap it down good with a bar of brown laundry soap. Place the paper soapy side down over those cracks around window frames to cut down on the winter breeze.

The water went off all over the city for several days because of a broken pipe. Though I always kept some water on hand, that time it wasn't enough. Afterwards, I kept my washing machine filled between washdays, so I'd always be prepared.

We never had running hot water, so washing hands or working at the kitchen sink in winter numbed my fingers. A Russian told us this joke:

Tourist: "I thought you said this hotel has hot and cold water."

Hotel Manager: "It does. We have hot water in the summer and cold water in the winter."

We heated our water on the stove. We all used the same bath water with an extra pan of boiling water added between each bather.

An icy fog hung over the city during the winter so it was useless to hang laundry outside. Clothes didn't dry; they simply absorbed the smell of coal smoke. I draped laundry all over the house, which contributed to a problem of condensation. Water dripped from the kitchen ceiling and our wallpaper mildewed.

I sometimes wondered, *what are we doing here, going through all this discomfort?* I looked forward to finishing our four-year term so we could get back to "normal." Then I'd read a passage such as 2 Corinthians 5.

Paul wrote, "We have as our ambition, whether at home or absent, to be pleasing to Him…the love of Christ controls us…He died for all, that they who live should no longer live for themselves, but for Him who died and rose again on their behalf…. God reconciled us to Himself through Christ, and gave us the ministry of reconciliation…."

And I remembered why we came.

Cory said, "A lot of people ask me, 'What do you like best here?'" He shook his head. "What is there to like? Of course, I can't tell them that. It's their home, and they're proud of it. But we're just coping all the time and there's no place to get away. Missionaries in other countries have nice hotels they go to, but we don't have anything like that. I keep thinking, what are we doing here? Sure, we've met some nice people, but it takes so much energy just to survive, and the task is so daunting."

A few days later, he told me at breakfast, "I had a strange dream last night. I went to a place with the best conditions possible for a missionary. I could even go fishing and play basketball. I was on an island that had everything you could ever want for making life comfortable, but there weren't any indigenous people! As soon as I arrived, I knew I'd made a mistake."

He took another bite of pancake. "I'm reading the book, *In His Steps*. The ultimate question is, 'What would Jesus do?' I know I don't always act like Him, or come close most the time, but the challenge to live for Jesus—even if it involves sacrifice—appeals to me. That's why I wanted to come to Ukraine. Serving Him is hard, but it gives purpose to life."

I learned two things about proper winter attire. Number one: going outside without a scarf is akin to going naked. If I forgot it at home, at least one person asked, "Why aren't you wearing a scarf?" Number two: you need a coat that covers your bottom. Cory had a heavy jacket, but strangers stared at him and friends asked if he was cold. I finally bought longer, heavier coats for all of us and snow pants for the girls.

Even with my warm boot-length coat, the old ladies wouldn't leave me alone. It was snowing lightly when I went to the market one day, but I felt toasty with my knit hat, hooded coat, boots, gloves, and scarf. An old woman grabbed me around my collar and scolded me for not having my top button fastened. She was from our church, but I didn't recognize her at the time.

I wrote home, "Don't worry about me, Mom. I have many mothers to take care of me."

Cory bought a fur hat made of nutria, a large rodent. I thought it stunk, but what do you expect of a dead rat? Cory noted, "It's only in countries where they don't need fur to keep warm that people are out to save the animals."

Most men wore fur hats. Some women wore stunning fur coats and hats. Though Ukraine contained much poverty, it had wealthy people too.

We rarely got snow, but when we did we borrowed our neighbor's sled. I pulled the girls around the courtyard, and they slid down a small snow-covered hill.

Housewives used fresh snow to "dry-clean" their rugs. After unrolling the rugs, they tossed snow on them and then swept off the dirty snow. Next, they hung the rugs on a bar and whacked them with a rug-beater.

Janelle and Alicia spent most days inside. Fortunately they usually got along and played well together. Sometimes they pretended they were Russian babushkas, or grandmothers. They wore big scarves and walked around the house saying, "*Kushet, kushet!*" Eat, eat!

Alicia, who liked to eat toothpaste, found a tube of deep-heat muscle ointment one day. A mouthful of that cured her.

Swans spent the winter at the Black Sea, so the girls and I took stale bread to feed them. Some waddled up on shore for their handout; others waited in the water for tossed tidbits. The braver ones took pieces of bread from my hand. If I held it just so, I didn't get my fingers nipped. Alicia wanted to try it too, but Janelle preferred to throw her bread on the ground.

Though beautiful, the swans had bad manners, especially when fighting for food. They pulled each other's feathers and bit each other on the neck. One swan looked like he'd eaten a pillow, with so much down stuck in his beak.

Seagulls made a terrible racket. They swooped down trying to snatch their share of free lunch. Pigeons paced back and forth with heads bobbing, seeking crumbs.

The girls looked forward to Christmas, but Janelle said she didn't want "the Ho Ho Ho Man" to come. Alicia decided she didn't want that noisy man either. Nothing like being traumatized by the jolly, fat man in red.

I found ornaments and lights at the market but no tree. With a chest cold, I lacked the strength to search much. I folded a green dishtowel in the shape of a triangle, pinned it to our wallpaper and decorated it instead.

They celebrate Christmas on January 7 in Ukraine. The biggest holiday is New Year's Eve. People decorate New Year trees and Grandpa Frost comes on New Year's Eve to bring gifts to children.

Russian tales say that Grandpa Frost and his granddaughter, Snow Maiden, live in a hut in the deepest woods of Siberia where they make gifts all year for good girls and boys. Stories vary on how he brings these gifts, perhaps on a sleigh pulled by a horse or deer, or he walks.

Snow Maiden always arrives first at parties for children. Young and kind, she is full of life and wears a long white gown. Grandpa Frost is old and can't walk very fast, so she encourages the children to call for Grandpa Frost.

Grandpa Frost wears big felt boots, like they wear in Siberia. He has a long white beard and wears a long, red coat lined with fur. He is stoutly built, like Russian men, not blubbery like his brother Santa who eats too many cookies.

We wanted to celebrate on December 25, keeping American tradition. It didn't feel the same, though, without the familiar rituals of the holiday season. December lacked Christmas programs and cookie exchanges and advertisements counting down the shopping days. In the absence of extended family, I valued Jesus as "Immanuel," or "God with us." He left the splendor and comfort of heaven for a stable much more dismal than our apartment.

Anya came dressed in her finest as our Christmas dinner guest. She pulled gifts from her sack before we ate: socks for Cory and me, ornaments and oversized underwear for the girls. I felt bad about her spending her meager funds on socks we didn't need, while she wore stockings with holes.

Our teammates had been in the U.S. and brought us a box of gifts from family members. Cory lost no time sniffing out a package of coffee, and I retrieved the baking powder. Ukraine was a good place to learn delayed gratification.

We doled out one or two gifts each day for a week—the girls got ultimate delight out of each one that way. Besides, we had only four pieces of Christmas paper and needed to reuse the paper to wrap each gift. The box was packed with love. The most exciting gift, though, may have been the box itself. I turned it over and made a toy stove and oven out of it using a felt pen and knife.

A truckload of Charlie Brown Christmas trees, scraggly pines, arrived in town on December 27. I got one and we decorated it as part of our ongoing celebration.

On New Year's Eve, Anya and Grandfather Frost came to our house around 9:00 p.m. to escort us to a New Year's Eve party. When we told Janelle that Santa Claus would come get us, she cried, "No Ho-Ho man! No Ho-Ho man!" until we explained it was just Maxim. She eyed him carefully when he arrived. Children shouted, cars honked, and people pointed at our escort.

Maxim, age seventeen, was the only teenage boy among girls in the youth group and came from a poor and troubled family. Anya took him under her wing, and he helped her teach Sunday School. He had shaggy hair until Cory invited him over for me to cut it.

We spent the evening with Luda, a newer believer, her husband and two children. Once a devout Communist, she had helped the KGB spy on Christians. During Soviet times, church members met in a different house every week to avoid detection, and she tried to find them so police could arrest them. She believed Christians were a menace to society and thought she was doing the right thing.

Shortly after the fall of the Soviet Union, she saw the *Jesus* film when a Russian evangelist showed it in Feodosia. She wept as she watched and gave her life to Christ. She said her life changed dramatically, since she used to drink and dance a lot. She worked full time to support her unemployed alcoholic husband and children but claimed, "Ever since I met Jesus, life isn't so hard."

New Year's Eve dinners are typically served late, and our first course didn't start until after 10:00 p.m. Anya had helped Luda prepare some ten different salads made in different combinations of onions, pickles, fish, peas, onions, beets, sour cream, potatoes, and…did I mention onions?

Luda's husband guzzled vodka before midnight, champagne afterwards and got louder and louder as the evening progressed. He tried to make his American guests feel at home by playing an old, warped tape of American rock music. With the TV also on, conversation was difficult.

We watched New Year's specials on television. Grandpa Frost passed out gifts. Firecrackers exploded outside at midnight. We started our second course, baked chicken, at 12:30. The girls stayed awake until after tea was served and we could finally go home around 2:00 a.m.

January is a month of celebration. New Year is its highlight. Christians honor Jesus' birth on January 7. On January 14, people celebrate the "Old New Year," though the calendar changed seventy years ago. Some say it simply provides another reason to get drunk.

Orthodox Christians commemorate January 21 as the day of Jesus' baptism. Many take water to the Orthodox church on this day to have it blessed by the priest. They save this holy water and drink it for sicknesses, apply it to wounds, and sprinkle it around the house in order to keep the devil out. They sprinkle the corners especially, since that's where the devil likes to hide. Some use the water to calm crying babies by washing the baby's face with it or by giving the child some to drink.

They keep a silver cross in the water. One person told me, "They believe that since it was blessed on this day, that's the reason why the water doesn't go bad. But I can put silver in any water and it won't go bad."

Tatiana told us that many years ago, people went caroling between Christmas and New Year. They sang outside the homes of friends and neighbors and received treats in return. After the Revolution, leaders forbade this practice, since many carols mentioned Christ or God.

Some children still go door to door around Christmas time, like American trick-or-treaters. I was quite unprepared when these children first came to our apartment. Some wore masks. Some showered me with barley. They recited a poem and then waited with bags held out. I passed on some of the abundant supply of candy the girls received with the holiday. Tatiana explained that the practice of wearing masks began as a way to scare away evil spirits in order to start the New Year right.

Our January highlight was the one-week visit of Larry Wren, a friend and the mission's pastor of a church in Wichita. He listened while we poured out our frustrations. He helped in the kitchen and read to Janelle and Alicia. They loved our houseguest.

His first night with us, Alicia called out around 2:00 a.m., "MAMA!"

I rushed to her room. "What is it?"

"I hear an animal in the living room…or a monster."

"Go back to sleep. That's just Larry snoring."

Larry gave us much encouragment. He reminded us how far we had come but said if we decided to return to the U.S. early, it wouldn't be failure. We felt grateful and relieved to know he cared about us more than our productivity.

He also met with church leaders to discuss an evangelistic outreach in March. An American music group planned to come, plus a speaker to talk on the theme of marriage and family.

"What is your biggest prayer request?" he asked us on his last day.

"I'd like to find a way to help the church reach out more," Cory said. "There are so many people who don't know Christ."

I answered, "I want to run the race with perseverance and my eyes on Jesus." Looking at anything else was too overwhelming. I felt inadequate to make any difference in the culture. We couldn't even keep our bathroom sink attached to the wall.

A winter storm had brought freezing rain about the time Larry arrived and cold temperatures kept the city in a blanket of ice all week. After he left, I woke in the night and thought I heard dripping outside. Was it my imagination? No, a warm front had moved in overnight and thawed out the city. The break in cold weather was wonderful.

I headed to our enclosed balcony to get potatoes, beets, and onions for borscht. The vegetables I had stored there had all frozen. I cooked up a big pot of potatoes, but they were bitter so I threw them all away.

Janelle and I were sick often with bronchial infections that first winter. I lay awake at night listening to Janelle cough, hoping and praying she would get better.

We had brought antibiotics and other medical supplies from the U.S., but many people shared their home remedies with us. One woman gave Cory a bundle of leaves, flowers, and other strange herbs. "Make tea with this," she said, "for Janelle's cough." Janelle wasn't impressed.

Anya suggested Janelle should put her head over a pot of boiled potatoes. Or we could give her a hot bath with mustard in the water, or put oil and mustard on her back and rub it in until she squirmed and complained, or put mustard in socks she wore at night.

Several women shared recipes guaranteed to cure a cough. Some suggested that warm milk with honey and butter added should do the trick. One warm milk recipe included chocolate, egg, and baking soda. Our neighbor advised vodka mixed with syrup. I would just smile and thank them.

Around bedtime one day, a church member showed up with a lump of sheep fat. She melted some in the kitchen and told me to rub it on Janelle's chest, back, calves, and the soles of her feet.

"Do that for ten days," she said, "plus give her warm milk with sheep fat added, and she'll get better."

Janelle screamed bloody murder. She wasn't going to let that woman rub sheep fat on her. I decided to stick with mentholated vapor rub. I figured she'd get better in ten days with or without sheep fat.

One older woman from the church brought several jars of home-canned fruit as medicine for Janelle's cough: cherries, apricots, pears, and plums. That's my kind of home remedy!

When I got sick, Anya brought meat gelatin. She made it from boiling a pig's head and said it was good medicine. I used it to make soup.

I learned various theories about how one catches a cold. Many told us a breeze through an open window would make us sick—even in ninety-degree weather. It's acceptable to go outside in the wind, but a breeze through a window is different. Sitting on cement, sitting on the floor, or sitting on the ground were also taboo, even in the summer, presumably causing sickness. When I had a sore throat, people asked, "Did you drink something cold?"

Strangers—especially older women—gave advice freely, adjusted my girls' clothing and rebuked me for not dressing them warmly enough. They tucked the girls' shirts into their pants, or told me to, so they wouldn't get sick from wind on their backs.

Whenever I bought something at the market, the vendor said, "Eat it in health" or "Wear it in health." Knowing that Ukrainians and Russians have always had harsh living conditions helped me understand this preoccupation with health. Those with strength survived.

When meeting on the street, acquaintances typically asked about the health of family members. After I stayed home sick from church one day, Giorgi called and asked, "How are you?"

I automatically chirped, "Fine."

"But aren't you sick?"

Russians want to know how you are when they inquire. It used to surprise me when strangers told me all about their aches and pains.

Under the Socialist system, the government provided free health care and many other benefits. The Soviet Union collapsed and the State could no longer provide all the benefits.

Under the new system, a person expecting treatment was required to bring all the needed supplies. For example, a patient with a broken bone had to bring bandages and plaster. Many people went without medical care simply because they could not afford it.

We heard of a man who felt everything during his five-hour operation because there was no anesthesia. Operating rooms were unheated and relatives had to bring food to the patient. Sometimes the patient went home to eat and bathe.

I tried not to think about the "what if" scenarios of a serious illness or accident. During those times of dread, I replayed the words of a missionary, Robyn Priest, who spent time in a remote part of Tanzania.

"Sometimes I wondered what we were doing there," Robyn had told me. "If any of us had needed emergency medical care, especially during the rainy season, it would have taken us days to get out. Then I realized the people we came to serve couldn't get out either, and they would never hear the gospel unless someone was willing to put up with a little mud."

Early in 1996, I read a report in the *Kiev Post*, an English language newspaper, about the state of health care in Ukraine. It said the Ukrainian government owed $70 million in back wages to health workers. The average health care worker earned $60 a month. Most had not been paid in months, so many doctors stopped going to work.

The article reported that in 1995, there were 274,500 deaths but only 4,500 births, the highest imbalance since World War II. Of the 4,500 live births, 45% were premature and 38% suffered birth defects—I assume a result of poor nutrition and alcohol. There were 900,000 abortions performed that year.

Right after Ukraine's independence in 1991, medicine could not be found at any price. With time, most medical supplies became available in pharmacies and kiosks. They were quite expensive, however, especially to people with low income who were used to getting them free.

We had a large box of medical supplies to give but didn't want the recipient to sell them. Tatiana had once been a patient at the cancer hospital where she noted their lack of supplies and saw how nurses brought medicine from home to give to patients. She suggested we might give to the cancer hospital.

When Cory and Igor delivered the medical supplies, the doctor seemed very grateful. We talked to Tatiana later about the contact. "He doesn't seem to mind working with the church or with Americans," Cory said.

Tatiana smiled. "Actually, when I first talked to him about the medicines, he was concerned about taking anything from the Baptist church."

Like Tatiana, he had once been a dedicated Communist. Can anything good come from a church, especially the Baptist sect? She assured him she had worked with this church for three years and found good people there.

Tatiana admitted, "I was also apprehensive when they first asked me to translate for Americans who came to work with the Baptist church. My husband didn't want me to have any dealings with the church, but we needed the money."

She told us of a popular movie shown some years earlier about a man who was beaten and forced to join a church. He eventually went mad. Consequently, many believe that people are forced to join non-Orthodox churches against their will—otherwise, why would anyone join such a sect? As a girl in school, Tatiana heard many rumors about the Baptist church: "They beat children. They eat children."

She said, "People who know I translate for the Baptist church have asked me, 'Have they converted you yet?' They are surprised when I tell them, 'No.'"

A few weeks later, she told us, "A nurse who works at the cancer hospital came to see me today. She said the new scalpels have been a big help in surgery, and they are telling patients the supplies and medicines were a gift from the Baptist church."

After years of slander, the church needed a better image.

Janelle and Alicia feeding swans at the Black Sea

Our first Christmas in Ukraine

A war memorial in Feodosia

I bought sour cream from the milk building at the market

We focused on learning Russian our first year

- 10 -
No Old Man on a Cloud

Tatiana continued to meet with us three times a week and tape-record words and phrases for us. We tried to sort out the male and female nouns with their matching verbs and adjectives. Since there's more to life than verb conjugations, we often used part of our Russian lesson to learn more about the culture.

When she was in school, teachers told her class, "Some grandmothers believe there is an old man with a long white beard sitting in the clouds watching us. How foolish! Our astronauts have been in outer space and they never saw God."

When studying art at a university not far from Moscow, she wanted to know more about the Biblical scenes on some old paintings, but nowhere in Moscow could she find a Bible for sale. There were, however, many books about why the Bible could not be true. From these books, she learned about the Bible. In one required course, "Scientific Atheism," the professor quizzed her about her beliefs before she could pass the course.

I found this very interesting and said, "If God is only make-believe, why do they work so hard to disprove Him? No one teaches against Santa Claus or fairies."

Tatiana shrugged. Cory told her of top scientists who became convinced in the existence of a Creator as they learned more about the universe, and we loaned her a book about weaknesses in the theory of evolution.

Modern newspaper stands openly sold pornography and summertime dress was surprisingly immodest. I asked Tatiana if she would attribute Ukraine's moral decline to the popular Western movies with sexual and violent content. Such movies and indecent attire had been prohibited during Soviet times.

She said the new Russian-made movies, regardless of topic, had nudity in them, and people with bad morals were heroes. She told of one popular film, which featured a prostitute who was a caring person. She lived a glamorous life, robbed from the rich, and gave to the poor. After this movie came out, girls on the street told a TV reporter they wanted to be prostitutes too but didn't know how to get this job.

During the Cold War, there were many movies about Americans starting a nuclear war. Tatiana was in high school then, and all girls received training as nurses in preparation for this great war with the U.S. I always thought the Russians wanted to start the war.

Tatiana never told her colleagues she gave private English lessons—or that she taught Americans Russian. "People have such a problem with jealousy," she said.

Still thinking as an American, I asked, "You mean like if someone gets a new car or a new house?"

"Oh no, nothing like that," she said. "If someone can afford better food...or a little nicer clothing, that's enough to make others jealous."

She told about an older woman she stayed with while studying in St. Petersburg. The well-to-do woman had nice crystal and china in her home. When she purchased a new dress, she bought an expensive dress and not just one, but two or three of the same dress—same size and same color. She said she didn't want people to be jealous of her. "They will say, 'Well, even though she has an expensive dress, she can afford only one.' I will know, however, that I can buy many dresses, and it gives me great satisfaction."

The Communists taught that no one should have more than someone else. Prosperous farmers had their land taken away after the socialist revolution. Under Communist rule, it was against the law for a family to own more than one cow and two goats.

Even today, those who stand out from the crowd are criticized. There is a Russian saying: "The tallest blade of grass is cut first."

If something good happens to a person or family, they don't tell others. Tatiana gave examples. "One family had a son who went to study in the U.S., but they kept it a secret. Another man told no one he was going to emigrate to the U.S. until the day before he left." She said that when others are jealous, people believe it can bring bad fortune.

I thought how different life is in the U.S., where we praise people who get ahead. Americans send out Christmas letters bragging about new cars, promotions, and trips to Europe.

"It stems from Stalin's time," she said, as though I should know what occurred.

I had to ask, "What happened then?"

For someone to be called an "enemy of the state" and executed, all that was necessary was for three witnesses to sign a paper charging a person with wrong. When someone was an "enemy of the state," his wife and close relatives were sent to Siberia, never to return. His children were left as orphans, and no one would help them, lest they be accused of helping an "enemy of the state." The man's property became ownerless and was distributed. So you needed only three jealous people who wanted someone's property for that person to be executed—good reason to keep a low profile and never accomplish much.

While discussing education with Tatiana, she spoke of discipline problems in Russian schools. "We have the same problem in America," I said. "So many kids are raised in daycare."

Tatiana raised her eyebrows. Soviet daycare was promoted as the ideal environment for raising children. She had always heard that if children spent too much time at home, they got spoiled. The educational philosophy under Communism stressed conformity and cooperation and sought to eliminate individuality. Parents simply don't know how to raise children properly.

Men and women alike were expected to work. Women received a two-year maternity leave, long enough to get the child potty trained. After that, children spent their days in group-care.

"When I think more about it," Tatiana said, "the better-behaved children are in Christian families, and those mothers stay home."

Igor visited the partner church in Kansas and after returning to Ukraine, he spoke at an evening church service about his impressions. American houses have a bathroom for every person. Big bathrooms. Some houses have more bathrooms than people living there. Most families have two cars or even more. Women don't have to work very hard. American kitchens are huge and have many appliances.

Everything he saw was so efficient and organized. One farm Igor visited was much bigger than collective farms in Ukraine but had only eight people working on it. People fly instead of going by train. Everything is clean: streets, sidewalks, public bathrooms, even farm tractors. Americans don't eat very much bread, but they eat a lot of meat. There are 300 churches in Wichita and they don't fight with each other.

People had a hard time believing it all and kept looking at Cory to see if he would nod and affirm what Igor said. It was so different from anything they had known they couldn't imagine it could be true. It must be something like heaven.

For years, Soviet authorities said the USSR was the most superior nation on earth. They claimed America was dirty, full of poverty and crime. Capitalism would soon fall. People had no reason to think differently.

Tatiana told us that when she was working on her thesis, she needed access to newspapers in English. After getting approval, she was allowed to see one communist paper from England. It wasn't enough so she sought further permission, got more signatures, and was finally allowed to see other newspapers but nothing more recent than five years old.

The saddest story I heard about censored access to the West was that after World War II, soldiers who served in other countries were not allowed to return to their homes. Authorities charged them with treason and placed them in concentration camps until they died. They had seen too much.

I doubt Communism can ever gain the same control it once had. People know too much now.

We invited Igor and his family over for dinner and he shared more impressions about his time in America. He could not understand why everyone smiled so much. Clerks, waitresses, everyone smiled.

I explained it's part of the job description. Conversely, we wondered why no one smiled in Ukraine, at least not in public.

Igor had been warned you must help yourself to food in American homes or else go hungry. Unlike Ukraine, no one will load up your plate or push food on you. In Ukraine, it is polite for a guest to take a very small portion when offered and proper for the hostess to load up the plate. Igor went hungry in the beginning, but it didn't take him long to catch on.

He was disappointed Americans pray so little, and he thought their posture wasn't respectful. In Ukraine one must stand or kneel when addressing the Almighty—no sitting allowed. Russian Christians pray both before and after a meal, and often before departing someone's home. They pray even before drinking tea.

Andre came to visit us during one Russian lesson so Tatiana could interpret everything. We first met Andre when he took us to see our teammates. We hadn't talked much since, though we saw him at church and heard him preach.

Andre said, "People are still talking and wondering why you left the comforts of America to move to Ukraine."

"We feel God has called us to Ukraine to help the church grow," Cory replied.

Andre said he also felt a call. When life was difficult and he felt like giving up in the ministry, he would look at his two-year-old son. After the death of their four-year-old girl, God confirmed that call and His love through the birth of two more children. He said it's good for a minister to have problems so they can relate to others who face difficulty.

"I want to work with you," Andre said, "and help you reach your goals. What do you want to do here?" Andre was the overseer for churches of Eastern Crimea, so we felt surprised and pleased by his offer.

"We don't want to start a ministry based on American ideas," Cory replied. "We want to support you in your work. What are your goals?"

Andre explained that he visited area churches and helped the ones with problems. "Many church leaders lack training," he said. "They get sidetracked on unimportant issues and neglect the message of salvation." Andre traveled by bus or hitchhiked. He was gone a lot and didn't see his wife and five children as much as he wanted.

Besides strengthening churches, Andre said he wanted to train leaders but didn't know how. He wanted to plant more churches but had no plan. He had received two years of training in Moscow but still didn't know how to start.

Cory said, "We also want to train leaders and plant churches."

"Do you want to work as a team?"

"Yes. We can't do it alone, especially since we don't know the language and culture very well. And we will be here a limited time."

We felt encouraged by the meeting, but nothing became of it for over a year. Perhaps the timing wasn't right for us then. We had been in Ukraine only seven months and had several more months to focus on learning Russian. Besides, we thought we came to work with the Feodosia church, not other churches.

Cory looked for ways to build a good relationship with Igor. He didn't want him to feel threatened by our presence or goals, and so he set up a meeting.

"I want to work with you, Igor," Cory assured him. "What are your goals for ministry?"

"I want to have a big church," Igor replied.

"How do you plan to do that?"

"I don't know. I've never had the freedom to plan for the future before."

"May I suggest something?"

Igor nodded.

"It's easy to spend a lot of time running around helping the old ladies. According to Ephesians 4, the job of the pastor is to equip other people for ministry. It would be good if you could come up with a ministry plan, something you can communicate to other people and get them to work on it with you. If I didn't have a goal and steps for reaching it, I wouldn't have a purpose for being here."

"That's a new idea. But I already have plans made for the year."

Cory thought Igor might not understand the difference between making plans and setting goals, so he talked about his hopes. He wanted to train leaders in evangelism and church planting. He acknowledged that he couldn't do much on his own and needed to work with local believers.

Later he told me, "Maybe I could encourage Igor to go to Melitopol for a couple days to talk with the pastor there. They went to school together. It might give him some new ideas for ministry. Sometimes people keep doing the same things just because they can't imagine anything else."

Anya quizzed me about the proper care and feeding of Americans. "Do Americans eat pork? Did you like that fish soup I made? Shall I heat water for them to bathe?"

Four people from Kansas planned to come that March to hold a marriage and family seminar in a public auditorium and Anya offered to host two ladies. The goal of the seminar was to help attract new people to the church.

I told Anya, "Americans aren't used to eating salad and borscht for breakfast. Bread and tea is enough, maybe with some cheese or an egg. The most important thing is to give them boiled water to drink."

Maxim helped Anya fix up her apartment. She told me afterwards, "I have a beautiful bathroom now, like yours."

I never knew my bathroom set a standard for beauty. Maxim had put up wallpaper and made a padded toilet seat by wrapping red plastic tape around some foam. "It's as soft as a sofa," she said proudly.

I couldn't tell her that few Americans actually *like* padded toilet seats. Our bathroom came furnished with a cushioned seat, made in Turkey. The plastic inside broke the first time we used it, but we couldn't find a better replacement.

The team arrived exhausted after the long flight and all-night train ride. One nice thing about hosting a short-term team was seeing how far we had come. We knew our way around and could translate conversations.

About 250 or 300 people came to meetings held in the rented auditorium. The speaker talked about marriage and family issues from a Christian perspective. Most interesting to me was the question/answer session at the end.

Questions reflected the local economic crisis, as well as the plight of people everywhere: "My husband doesn't work, I do, and we fight about money all the time."

"My kids think I'm old fashioned."

"My spouse is abusive."

"My children don't appreciate all I've done for them."

"By what sign of the zodiac can I find a good mate?"

Instead of inviting people to accept Christ at the meeting, church leaders thought it was better to call on those interested in learning more about Jesus. Eleven people gave their names and addresses.

I invited the Kansas team over for dinner. Whenever we had company, I wished the kitchen wasn't so isolated from the rest of the house, since I couldn't hear any conversation as I finished meal preparations. When we visited someone else's home, we rarely saw the hostess. While we sipped soup, she mashed potatoes. While we ate potatoes, she prepared tea.

Joining the team for dinner, I listened to their impressions. "The people here are so hospitable," said one. "They don't have much, but they feed us so well."

"I didn't expect so much poverty and dirt," said another. "The buildings remind me of the housing projects in inner-city Chicago."

"But it seems safer here; many people go walking at night."

One team member joined me in the kitchen after dinner. She watched me heat water on the stove and kept me company while I washed dishes.

"How do you live here?" she asked. "Do you like it? Or...ah...are you content? Maybe that's a better way to put it."

Fair question—how should I answer? "I guess feelings don't have anything to do with it," I said finally. "We are here because we are supposed to be. Some days, it's hard to get out of bed to a cold house, but the girls need to eat breakfast. I need to shop. I need to cook and clean. We need to study Russian so we can understand what's going on around us."

I told her I often thought of a devotional I had read by Elizabeth Elliot. She said that people often focus too much on how they feel, instead of simply doing what they need to do in spite of how they feel. By simply "doing the next thing," she walked her way out of many pits of despair. Following her philosophy helped me cope.

Though I enjoyed the American fellowship, I was still fighting the flu and didn't have energy to spend much time with them. As they drove away, I stood with Anya, Maxim, and Lena. Anya looked at me and, drawing lines down her cheeks, asked, "You don't cry?"

The team had been in Feodosia about ten days. I knew it was time for them to return to their lives and time for us to get on with ours. "The Americans left," I said, "But I'm a Russian woman." They laughed.

"Thank you for living with us," Lena said.

Going on a short-term trip is something like a quick plunge in the Arctic Ocean. It's an adventure, maybe even life changing. Visitors can take pictures and tell friends at home about the incredible experience. It's quite another matter to make the Arctic home, to discover its beauty and live with the dangers.

I know God doesn't call everyone to live in "the Arctic." Nevertheless, I was glad some would take a quick plunge. They brought skills we didn't have, enthusiasm, and chocolate chips.

Quite a few visitors attended church the Sunday after the evangelistic outreach. We saw no one greet them, however, except for Stefan.

"It really bothers me," Cory told me later. "These people are obviously searching and want to know more about Christ. I'm frustrated, because God wants all people to know Him, but the church sets up so many barriers. These church people can't seem to think in terms of friendships and trying to influence people for Christ."

When a guest visits a Ukrainian or Russian home, the host family is extremely hospitable. They give the guest the best slippers, the best chair, and the best food. It seemed as though the church should be that way, but years of oppression taught Christians to be suspicious of visitors instead of welcoming.

The doorbell rang. It was Anya. She sat down on the couch and in tears poured out her frustrations with the church. Because she was a newer believer and not part of the core group, she didn't feel accepted. She gave much time and energy to her work with youth and children.

Neverthcless, some people said she was a bad influence because she wore lipstick and therefore shouldn't work with youth. "Please start a new church," she begged.

We encouraged her to forgive and work out her struggles with the people involved. We knew the church had problems, but none is perfect. We thought Feodosia needed another church, or many more, but didn't think we should start one. We didn't want to plant an American church, patterned after our culture and dependent on us to lead it.

A few days later, Cory came home excited after a visit with Stefan. They had a growing friendship and mutual respect. Cory finally knew enough Russian for deeper discussions with him. "We had a wonderful talk," he told me. "I wish my conversations with Igor were that good."

Cory thanked Stefan for talking to visitors at church Sunday. Stefan told him he wanted to reach new people for Christ but knew the church was slow to accept newcomers. "The church has had these problems as long as I've been here," he said. "Many Christians don't read the Bible. They hang on to their traditions as a substitute."

Cory suggested, "Maybe we can start a parallel work—let the old church keep its traditions and start a new congregation with an evangelistic focus."

Stefan said they once considered starting a new church, but the idea was quickly struck down. Though he saw the value of a separate group, he thought they couldn't start one without causing hard feelings.

"So what do you want to do?"

Stefan spoke of his desire to be involved with evangelism, even if he had to go to outlying areas. As he talked, he became more and more excited. He could go to villages and show the *Jesus* film.

Church leaders did follow up on the eleven people who turned in their names and addresses at the family seminar. Igor visited them and held special meetings on Sunday evenings. He answered their questions, and they watched a Dobson film translated into Russian.

Over the next few weeks, some of them came forward to confess their sin at the end of the service. They knelt in front and prayed from the heart. Some sobbed as they prayed. Many in the congregation wept quietly, witnessing their heartfelt confessions. Igor presented each with a new Bible. Over time, however, the newcomers stopped attending.

I met a woman at the family seminar who taught English in a village school. She also tutored her sixteen-year-old daughter in English and hoped her daughter could talk to real live Americans. She lived about one-

and-a-half hours by train outside Feodosia and asked if she and her daughter might visit us some Sunday after church.

Several weeks later, they surprised me by showing up at church in Feodosia. Instead of listening to the sermon, I struggled. I knew I should invite them home for lunch but thought of our poorly-stocked refrigerator and untidy house.

I remembered those books I had read on hospitality. Hospitality isn't impressing guests with gourmet cooking and flawless housekeeping. It doesn't apologize for what you don't have but offers what you have to make the guest feel welcome. It's other-centered, not self-centered. I decided I could warm up that leftover borscht.

After the service, I sent Cory and the girls home to clear away breakfast dishes and other Sunday-morning-dash-to-church rubble while I waited to walk with our guests. They stayed all afternoon. The mother said she had many students who didn't attend class in her village. If she gave them a bad mark, she got in trouble with her superiors who said, "Visit the pupils' homes and make them attend class." If she gave bad students passing grades, no one bothered her.

She attended church in her village but thought church members didn't really like her since she was better educated. Nevertheless, she planned to get baptized that summer when the sea was warm enough.

- 11 -
He Is Risen Indeed

By April, I could see that spring had finally come. We still wore multiple layers, but on sunny days I could open our windows to air out the apartment. I found buds on trees and flower foliage almost six inches high. The swans wintering at the Black Sea had disappeared. Perhaps the most telling sign of all: we found four big, ugly cockroaches!!! (I should have counted my blessings those cold winter months.)

The price of fall produce—carrots, cabbage, and apples—doubled, but the price of eggs and milk dropped some. I found green onions and parsley at the market, glad to get some greenery back in our diet.

With Easter approaching, we asked Tatiana to tell us more about Easter customs in Ukraine. The season started in mid-February with a week for eating pancakes and butter. Then began forty days of Lent during which all good Orthodox Christians give up eating meat..

On Palm Sunday, people take pussy willow branches to the church for decoration. The last three days before Easter are a complete fast. Saturday night, the Orthodox believers hold an all-night service. On Sunday, people greet strangers on the street with, "He is risen," and hear the reply: "He is risen indeed." The Communists outlawed this greeting, but "foolish" old folks held on to their hope.

Egg dying is considered an art and women paint elaborate designs on boiled eggs. Tatiana made her dye from onion skins and used leaves for decorative designs.

Children play games with boiled eggs. Each has a boiled egg. They pair off and hit eggs together. The person with an unbroken egg in the end wins.

On the Sunday following Easter, many go to the graveyard and eat boiled eggs at the grave of deceased loved ones. They visit with friends at neighboring gravesites and eat more boiled eggs. It's a big social event.

The eggs are a sign of new life, Tatiana explained. And yes, even during communist times, people followed this tradition; they gathered at the tomb with hope in the Resurrection.

One church member invited us to his home to "get cleaned up for Easter" in the sauna he had built. When we arrived, his wife ushered us to a small wood-lined room with a wood stove in it. She instructed us to sit in the hot room for a while, take a cold shower, and repeat the process several times. One hour of baking and showering seemed long enough for me, but they asked why I did it so fast.

We invited Giorgi's two daughters and Igor's two girls over to help dye Easter eggs using an egg-dye kit from the U.S. They had never dyed eggs before; that is an art reserved for mothers and grandmothers. Nor had they ever hunted for Easter eggs, but they quickly caught on. In Ukraine, people exchange Easter eggs as gifts. After an hour of being hunted and hidden and dropped, our eggs weren't gift material. They made good egg salad though.

In honor of Easter, I bravely exchanged my winter boots for dress shoes. I let the girls wear shoes, too, and double stockings instead of pants with their dresses. They skipped like colts out to pasture.

We had Easter dinner at the home of a family with three teenage girls. Janelle thought the slices of pig fat were cheese. Nope. I choked hers down with a piece of bread after she rejected it. Alicia ate three slices and wanted more. We dined on cabbage soup, meat gelatin, and garlic bread, plus mashed potatoes and meatloaf patties.

Our hosts grew medicinal herbs and sold them at the market. They served us bitter herb tea and before we left, they gave us a packet of foul smelling flowers—for curing a cough—along with jars of pickles and cherry jam.

On the way home, Janelle told me, "You're a better cooker, Mama."

Anya continued to tell us long tales about those in the church who didn't treat her right. Igor told us not to listen to her and told her not to talk to us, but we didn't need her stories to know there were problems.

It's natural, I suppose, that when a church or group gets someone new who is perceived as having some clout, discontented folk will gather 'round to fill those ears with tales of what's wrong. Anya relayed more than her share.

I told her to forgive, but her anger continued to burn. She possessed a strong sense of justice; bitterness kept her wounds infected. She collected complaints from others and added them to her own list. I told her to talk to the people concerned.

"I've done that and it doesn't do any good," she said. We knew we couldn't fight her battles.

"Then pray for those people," I replied. "And maybe God wants to show you your own faults. It's easy to say other people are wrong and not see your own sin."

Cory sensed a growing tension in his relationship with Igor. "I don't mind working on the building; the hardest part is dealing with Igor. When I try to talk to him, even to encourage him, he gets defensive. I'm the foreigner and he tells me, 'You don't understand.' That's probably true, but I'm trying to understand. I want to help him, but he is so suspicious."

"We're outsiders with new ideas," I said. "He sees us as a threat."

"I really don't think we're undermining him in any way. I've asked him some hard questions. I know we won't always agree, but I'm trying not to usurp his authority or gain a following of my own. I think I've avoided that."

He learned that some people who had asked his opinion had gone to Igor, taken his words out of context, and said, "Cory thinks we should do it this way." Cory decided to meet with Igor and Stefan to clear the air and discuss other business.

"I'm trying to support him," he told me. "I hope that once he sees it, he will relax a bit."

We met at our house while the girls napped. Cory started by saying, "This isn't our culture, so we will make mistakes we don't even know about. We ask your forgiveness and we want you to correct us. We come from a different culture, so we will have a different way of looking at some things. People will sometimes misinterpret what we say. We don't want to cause problems for you or for the church."

Igor drew a picture of a boiler room, a pipe, and a house. He labeled the boiler room as the church council, the pipe as communications, and the house as the congregation. "There will always be some pressure on the pipe," he said. "A kink in the pipe adds more pressure—pressure that can lead to a blowout. You are that kink in the pipe. You will feel pressure from both sides as long as you try to be friends with both sides."

He mentioned Anya. I told him what I'd told her, so he'd know we weren't eating up everything she said. He visibly relaxed.

With that behind us, Cory started on another topic. "You know we came here as part of your partnership with Wichita. The church in Wichita gave money for the building project, but the goal for the partnership was to help you do more evangelism. That's why we came. I'd like you to think about how we can help you in the best way. You don't need to answer right now, just think about it."

"What did you think about what he said?" Cory asked me later. "About being a 'kink in the pipe?'"

"I read an article on culture shock that said missionaries aren't the only ones who experience it. The locals do too when they are exposed to different ideas, especially ideas which bring about or require change. Even positive changes are stressful."

"I'm trying to move slowly and tone down my expectations."

"I know."

"Regarding being in the middle, quite a few people at church told me they like the way I'm friendly with everyone. I get along with church council members, at least most of them, and the others in the congregation too."

Though Cory attended every church service, I found it difficult to attend even once a week. It was hard to worship in a different language among those who cherished different customs. I felt the loneliest on Sunday morning—like an outsider—and it took so much effort to build relationships. Knowing about the problems affected my attitude, too.

As I made my way to an empty spot on a bench one Sunday, I stopped to greet several old ladies along the way. One elderly woman seemed so pleased to see me. Her kind face broke into a thousand wrinkles when she smiled. Her bright eyes expressed concern. She asked about my health and about the girls.

"Thank you for living with us," she said, clasping my hand in both of hers.

I felt hugged. I still couldn't understand all of the hymns and sermons, but Jesus was there and I belonged to His body.

Anya came to visit us the next day. She said she had been terribly depressed the last few days and then a light came on. She apologized, with tears, for speaking negatively about church leaders. "I realized criticism is like a curse," she said. "It opens a door for Satan to cause problems. I should pray for them instead." I felt like singing.

Warmer weather made it easier to go for walks. While taking the girls to the sea, we passed a public bathhouse. We occasionally saw young soldiers standing outside—teenagers with short haircuts and uniforms—waiting for their turn. Janelle and Alicia were afraid of those soldiers even though they carried no guns.

Many military personnel lived in Feodosia. I heard that when the Soviet Union was intact, one-third of Feodosia's population had been military. Feodosia was a closed city then, meaning no foreigners could visit, and Soviet citizens needed a special pass.

Janelle and Alicia had seen an Easter drama in Kansas the previous year and decided soldiers are very bad people because they hit Jesus. When they played together, the "bad guys" were either soldiers or Pharaoh. We explained that not all soldiers are bad. "Even Uncle Mike used to be a soldier, and Igor and Giorgi were too."

After this discussion, Janelle eyed the group outside the bathhouse and declared, "Those are good soldiers. They didn't hit Jesus."

May Day was once an important communist holiday. An old Russian-English dictionary I found at the market said, "On May Day, working people of the whole world display their solidarity." During Soviet times everyone got a two-day holiday. Red flags flew all around town. Flowers decorated the statue of Lenin.

Anya invited us to attend the May Day parade. As we walked to the parade site near the train station, she tried to explain the significance of May Day.

"It first started in Chicago in early 1900s," she said.

Chicago? Oh, she must be referring to the beginning of labor unions in America.

"They told us in school how the oppressed American workers united against evil capitalism. Our teachers said capitalism would soon fall, making way for communism."

The parade had no floats, no marching bands, and no horses. Elderly folk held red banners with slogans such as: "Solidarity for the Working People." Some had pictures of Lenin or red flags with the communist hammer and sickle. Others carried flowers, which they laid at the feet of Lenin's statue. War veterans marched in uniform.

An older man stood beside us wearing a faded green suit with war ribbons on his chest. A tear ran down his weathered cheek. He told us, "I fought with my friend against Germany in World War II. Many died on the front lines. We risked our lives to make our country great...not for this. My friend died yesterday because he had no food to eat."

Anya told him, "The country is in a mess because people haven't followed God."

A smaller group came at the end of the parade, holding anticommunist signs—younger people, businessmen.

At our next Russian lesson, Tatiana commented, "The warmer weather puts everyone in a good moods, but pensioners are still concerned. They didn't get their pension last month, and few of them have anything to live on." The town council spent the money planting flowers and painting buildings in preparation for May Day and the upcoming tourist season.

I had been sick a lot during the winter, and even in the spring I fought a reoccurring chest cold. As a result, I rarely went out except for trips to the market and didn't visit people much, saving my energy for the labor-intensive housework. Since I couldn't get out much, the girls didn't either.

Janelle and Alicia talked daily about Oregon, their cousins and grandparents. "How many days will we stay here? I want to go to 'Bekah's house." I heard it often.

They knew it was a long way to cousin Rebekah's house. I used to say, "We will go see them when you get bigger." Then I thought they might feel punished somehow for being too small, so I just told them we came to Ukraine to tell people about Jesus.

One night Janelle said, "We are here to tell people about God, like Jonah went to Nineveh. After Jonah told people about God, then what did he do? Did he get to go home again?"

"Yes," I said, "He went back to see his friends."

Janelle said, "My friends miss me *very much!*"

Separation from family wasn't so hard when I didn't have children.

It seems Feodosia has two seasons: winter and summer. Once it warms up, it gets hot fast. I didn't look forward to the extreme heat but felt relieved to be warm once again. I found more signs of spring: lettuce, radishes, and green onions in the market. After washing the mud off every lettuce leaf, I relished the greenery and crunch.

Perhaps it was the fresh produce or the warmer weather, but I soon felt better than I had in a long time. With new energy, the girls and I walked to Giorgi's house to visit his wife, Luba, and their children. I hadn't been there for months. I left our dishes unwashed and the house in disarray, but woman cannot live by housework alone.

We had a wonderful visit. Janelle and Alicia played with new kittens, rode the neighbor's swing and inspected the chickens. I learned what to do with those sour-tasting greens I'd seen at the market: make green borscht with them. I talked with Luba while she cooked.

She spoke of how Christians were discriminated against when she was growing up. While walking to church as a child, she always hoped she wouldn't see any classmates. Teachers mocked her and her siblings since they were Christians. Classmates called them bad names. I didn't understand all her words but understood enough to know it was miserable and fearful for her as a child to be from a Christian family.

We ate green borscht, watched cartoons, and got a tour of the garden. The girls ran all the way home. That night they forgot to ask, "When can we go to Oregon?"

Missionaries in the city of Kherson told me about a spring retreat in Odessa for women missionaries. They also invited Cory to attend a seminar on Islam, scheduled to take place before the women's retreat. Yippee, I'd get an outing!

The seminar Cory attended in Kherson gave him the chance to mingle with men from other parts of Ukraine and see what they were doing. He met some enthusiastic Russian evangelists and pastors. Some wanted to work among the Tatar, an unreached people group in Crimea. "It was a great seminar," he said. "It helped me think through my strategy some more."

Cory and the two male missionaries in Kherson took over childcare after their seminar while the ladies headed to Odessa. We stayed at a former campground for Young Pioneers, a Communist club. Though not exactly a four-star hotel, the facilities were adequate and located on the beach. About thirty women gathered from different parts of Ukraine. I enjoyed worship in English, pizza, and fellowship with women from my culture.

We went to Ukraine for the people of Ukraine, but it takes a lot of work to build relationships cross-culturally. It goes beyond trying to communicate in a new language. I wondered if I was doing something offensive. Was I dressed okay? Was I smiling too much? I could relax when spending time with those who play the relationship game with the same set of rules.

The speaker talked about Abraham's walk with God. God required sacrifices of Abraham but blessed him along the way. She encouraged the women to list things they have given up.

Ideas flowed freely: family, friends, ability to communicate, comforts, adequate health care. Some told stories with an edge of resentment.

As I looked at my list of "things sacrificed," I realized I haven't truly surrendered those things until I could say with Paul, "I consider everything like rubbish compared to the surpassing value of knowing Christ."

Giant statues of "Father" Lenin remain

Bitter Water Made Sweet

Janelle and Alicia liked to throw rocks in the water on our walks to the Black Sea. With the warmer weather, they waded out and tossed pebbles back on shore, as though stocking up on ammunition for fall and winter.

Returning from an afternoon walk one day, the girls and I met our neighbor, Katya, on the landing outside our door. This young mother was platinum blond when we first met, became a redhead and then brunette—greasy brunette.

"Come in," she urged. We stepped into the small apartment across from ours and saw she already had company. It was her daughter's second birthday.

Their bedroom doubled as a dining room and living room. The place smelled like urine, since their girl still wasn't potty trained and they didn't use diapers. A table stood before the bed—dinner was served.

I sat on slightly damp blankets next to Grandma and Grandpa. The father poured vodka into crystal shot glasses for a toast to the health and happiness of little Vera.

"I'll have juice," I said. I decided to pass on the chicken too, noticing there weren't enough pieces to go around. "We've already eaten."

The children soon got up from the table. Vera kept tackling Janelle and Alicia—to their distress—but they soon settled into a happy game of hide-and-seek. They climbed back and forth through a hole in the bedroom door, where a piece of opaque glass should have been.

Grandpa picked a wet pair of girl's pants off the floor and wiped his hands. Then he wiped his mouth and passed the soiled pants around. I wondered if he had too much vodka, but others followed his example.

How do you "love your neighbor as yourself" when you don't even like them?

The next afternoon, Katya brought Vera over to play and stayed to talk. Vera kept grabbing whichever toys Janelle and Alicia held. I finally suggested we could go for a walk. The girls were stressed and I didn't want Vera wetting on our carpet. I also wanted some fresh air, since neither mother nor daughter had apparently had a bath for a while.

Katya dashed home to change into nice clothes and we walked to the sea, where the girls threw pebbles in the water. A stiff breeze blew, but several children swam and two large women suntanned in their underwear. They looked as though they had been faithful sun-worshipers their fifty or sixty-odd years.

"Sun tanning is good for your health," Katya said. "It will keep you from getting sick the next winter."

Katya's husband joined us at the waterfront. Conversation turned to the troubled economy. Though his salary was six months late, he bought candy for the girls. I wished he hadn't.

Our friendly neighbor, Anna, invited the girls to come see her baby chicks. Anna shared a wall with us, so she always knew what kind of day we were having. She had a garden spot a twenty-minute walk away and planned to put her chickens there, but meanwhile, she kept the chicks on her enclosed balcony.

Janelle and Alicia were delighted. Alicia wanted to hold them. Janelle said later she wanted to have a baby chick too—but not one that gets big.

Most people tasted milk before buying it at the market. Since I heeded warnings about drinking raw milk, I smelled it instead.

One milk lady was also selling flowers. I took a good whiff of her milk but could only smell flowers. It looked good, so I took it. I got home and discovered I had purchased goat milk. Cory was not impressed.

Could I disguise it? I made pudding and gravy and pancakes—and discovered there is no way to disguise goat milk. Cory said, "It's still like gagging on Billy goat hair."

Vladimir Alexandrovich—a tall, thin man with thick glasses and gray hair—was the chief greeter at church. He hadn't been a Christian very long but stood outside every Sunday morning, no matter what the weather, welcoming people as they came through the gate. He worked as a garbage collector and used his free time to help widows in distress.

One day Vladimir recruited Cory to help him cut grass at an old widow's house. The 45-minute walk took them up a hill on the outskirts of town to a run-down shack.

Though poor, the 88-year-old owner kept her home tidy. She had a small garden, two goats, and a plot of knee-high grass. She pointed out two scythes for cutting winter hay for her goats.

For the next two-and-a-half hours, Cory and Vladimir hacked away. It took Cory a while to get the swing of things, but his sickle actually cut, as long as he sharpened it every other row.

The old woman was so grateful, she wanted to give the men some goat milk to take home. Cory declined her kind offer.

Though Cory came home with new muscles and blisters, the trip gave him good one-on-one time with Vladimir Alexandrovich. Cory came to do "leadership development" in Ukraine and decided the most valuable discussions might not take place in a classroom but on the road.

During summer months, the population of Feodosia tripled in size as Russian tourists came to vacation at the Black Sea. Many locals earned money for the rest of the year by renting out rooms or selling produce.

The pebbled beach was covered with a carpet of humanity, with person after person lying in the sun trying to collect enough vitamin D to last through cold Russian winters. I didn't like crowds, but the girls loved to paddle around with their swim rings and shovel pebbles with beach toys.

Old women at church scolded me constantly for being so white. I'd tell them, "If God wanted me to have dark skin I would have been born in Africa." They smiled. We visited the beach late in the afternoon, to avoid the intense midday sun.

Russian toddlers wore nothing at all at the beach, for a complete tan. Janelle and Alicia played in their underwear, like the older children. Large women wore bikinis, tanning their bulges without shame. Russian swimsuits seemed to be "one size fits all."

American women have been tormented by fad-diet plans for so many years, they believe, "If I could just lose ten more pounds, I'd look better." Many old ladies in Ukraine told me I was much too thin. "Life here must be too hard on you," they said.

During the winter, I started to believe them. I thought if I could just add about ten more pounds, I'd be much warmer. I never learned to like raw pig fat though, so I started to add sour cream to everything.

The sidewalk scales disappeared during the winter but returned with warm weather. I paid the attendant twelve cents, stood on a scale, and got my weight in kilograms. Apparently, my aerobic workout washing clothes and the four-flight "Stairmaster" to our apartment made up for the extra sour cream.

We got the occasional letter that said, "Your life must be so exciting," but even missionaries have routine. Life was easier in the summer, but I still had to collect water for the regular shortages, walk to the market, and pick rocks from my rice. With fresh fruit coming on, I carried extra loads and canned to give our diet more variety in the winter.

My trip to the market took me by garbage piled in an alley awaiting collection. Ancient trucks and overloaded buses passed me, coughing black exhaust. A woman sweeping the sidewalk threw dust in the air with the broad strokes of her twig broom. I tried not to breathe as I passed her, but the dust stuck to my face.

Reaching the market, I scanned the produce and loaded my bags for the return trip. In front of our apartment, water gushed from cracks around a manhole cover. It smelled like sewer. I carefully stepped around the foul-smelling liquid that poured into the street. It ran this way for a couple days every week or so, until someone came to fix it.

Our entryway smelled like urine, since desperate passersby used it as a toilet. The cement stairs were cracked and dirty, and we often found used hypodermic needles littering the landings. I didn't like climbing to the fourth floor with all our groceries, but I was grateful we lived high enough to get some fresh air.

Cory came home grumbling after a day of painting, "I asked Igor again how the church can do more outreach. He says we need to focus on the church building first. I think my biggest frustration is not knowing how God will use us here. We can be busy with many good things, but that isn't my goal. I want to accomplish something with a long-term impact. I believe God wants to do more too."

I served dinner and let him talk. Our year for language learning was almost over. We had better insight into the culture and had built some good relationships but still didn't know how to help the church grow.

"I see so many ways the church could be involved in ministry," he continued, "but they just don't see them. I'd like to do more, but we're just surviving."

A former missionary at our home office, David Giles, wrote to us, "Most missionary work is not soaring on wings as eagles, nor running without being weary. If you can walk and not faint, even that is a great accomplishment."

I woke up one morning with a thought out of nowhere. No, it must have been from God. When the people of Israel came to bitter water, Moses did something so they could drink it. What did he do?

I lay there for a moment to ponder. Did he hit it with his rod? Or throw salt in it, or a branch? I didn't have time to look it up, so while making breakfast and going to the market and canning cherries, I wondered. I thought of circumstances I didn't like, situations that made life in Ukraine hard to swallow. I made a mental list. What was God trying to say? Could He still turn bitter water into sweet?

While the girls napped, I looked it up. Exodus 15:25 "Then he cried out to the Lord, and the Lord showed him a tree; and he threw it into the waters, and the waters became sweet."

I thought of another tree, the cross of Jesus. I wrote down everything I didn't like in Ukraine and thought, *How does the cross apply to this? Can the cross make my bitter waters sweet?*

- Inconveniences: It wasn't convenient for Christ to leave heaven and die for us.
- Sporadic water: Jesus said, "I thirst."
- Crowds at the market: Jesus died for them.
- Carrying heavy bags home from the market: Jesus carried a cross.
- Language barrier: Jesus left a position of power to become a helpless baby.
- The dirt and smells: Jesus left a place of beauty for a sin-ruined world. He walked dusty roads and lived in cities without indoor plumbing.
- Separation from family: Jesus was separated from the Father, so we might have fellowship.
- Mundane housework: Jesus was homeless.
- Some don't accept us: Not everyone liked Jesus.
- The way I take out my frustrations on my husband and girls: Jesus died so I could be forgiven.

I knew Jesus called us to pick up our cross to follow Him but decided I should focus more on the cross of Christ instead of my own. Jesus suffered more than I ever will.

Jesus had a bitter cup to drink too but for the joy set before Him, He endured the cross. He didn't focus on His misery but on the reason why He went through it all—people. *Lord, give me a greater love for people.*

I saw two sides to the cross: His suffering and His love. He loves people in general, but He also loves *me.* When Jesus commanded us to "Go into all the world and preach the Gospel," He promised to be with us until the very end.

Later I tried to tell Anya about my inspiration, how looking at the cross makes our difficulties easier. She looked at me strangely and said, "But that's normal life for us: carrying food from the market, interrupted water. Besides, you and I have it easier than people who live in villages. We have a faucet in our kitchen. We have an indoor toilet."

Anya was probably my best friend in Ukraine, but our backgrounds were so different. There were things she just couldn't understand. On the other hand, perhaps contentment is mostly a matter of perspective, with whom you compare yourself.

Cory found encouragement and new perspective for his journey too. He told me, "I've been reading about Joseph in the book of Genesis. Joseph had a sense of call, but he ended up in prison. He tried to get out, but God had a reason for it and the timing wasn't right. I need to be patient too."

When Cory and Stefan went to Simferopol to get our visas renewed again, I went along and took the girls. I wanted to go shopping in "the big city" and spend time with an American woman I'd met at the ladies' retreat.

We had lived in Ukraine almost one year, but this was my first trip to Simferopol, not counting the day of our arrival. The sixty-mile trip took two hours and I admired the scenery along the way. I felt like a shut-in let out for a Sunday drive. Janelle and Alicia exclaimed every time they saw a cow. Janelle asked if we were in Oregon.

Simferopol contained bigger stores, taller buildings, and more beggars. The apartments had elevators, hot water, and heat during the winter. The missionaries I came to visit took me to a store with imported food. I was excited to find cornflakes, since I missed cold cereal.

Meanwhile, Cory had his encounter with the visa official, a former KGB head with an intimidating manner. We got approval for three more months, but the ordeal was as stressful as usual.

Bitter water made sweet—Roman officials treated Jesus even more harshly.

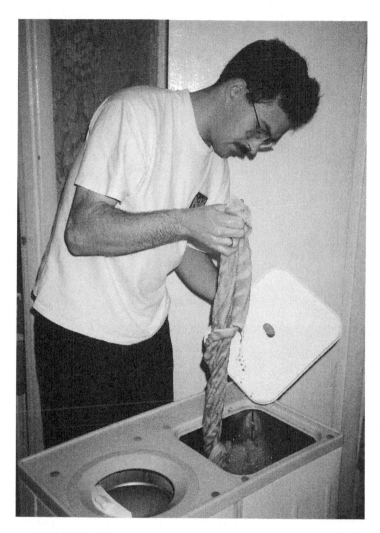

Our Russian washing machine with centrifuge

Bread kiosk

Dried fish

- 13 -
Now What?

The church planned to hold a day camp for their children and those from non-Christian homes. Igor invited Cory to help Anya plan the program. Teens in the church would help lead the camp.

Cory held a seminar for the young leaders and taught on Biblical leadership. He stressed that a leader is one who serves, as Christ did. After his first session, he told me, "That was really fun. It was hard, since I taught in Russian. I know I butchered the language, but they seemed to understand me okay. Maybe this seminar and the camp will give Igor a little more confidence in what I can offer. Maybe it will be a good starting point for doing more leadership training."

The next day he said, "I got to talk with Igor today. I suggested we could develop small groups as a way to follow-up on people after the festival in October, and maybe I could help him train group leaders. He said it was a good idea, but the other brothers would never go along with it, because it broke tradition. I need to spend more time with these guys."

Cory began informally discipling one teenager, Maxim. He had been our "Santa Claus" escort to a New Year's party and was a regular guest at our table. I think food at his own home was rather scarce.

Maxim, age seventeen, was the only Christian in a destitute family. His mother and older brothers drank heavily. One brother had died two months earlier, soon after he came home from prison. He had received many beatings and became very sick at the prison.

One day after dinner Maxim told us, "God woke me up three times last night and said I should teach." He had been helping Anya with Sunday School and wanted to study youth ministry. His face glowed when he received application forms for a Bible college in Ukraine.

Four Americans came to help with the camp. They brought fresh ideas, enthusiasm, and equipment. A father and son from Kansas, Darcy and Vance, stayed with Stefan. The two women stayed with us. We had always stopped at June and Susanne's house when we needed a bed on our way through Eugene and finally returned the favor.

June soon became a combination of human trapeze and Mother Goose for Janelle and Alicia. They swung on her arms, stopping only to sit on her lap with a pile of books. They loved the extra attention.

Over ninety children, ranging in age from seven to twelve, attended the week-long day camp. More than half came from non-Christian homes. They sang, heard Bible stories, played games, ate lunch, did crafts, and swam in the sea. Several expressed surprise that a Christian program could be so much fun. For many, it was the first time to hear about Jesus.

One nine-year-old girl, Lena, came to the camp with dirty, infected sores on both hands. She seemed scared and kept her head down. Anya said she came from a destitute home with drunken parents. June, a nurse, tenderly treated her wounds and gave her antibiotics. Over the week, she blossomed.

On the final day she asked, "I come back tomorrow, right?"

"No, there's no camp tomorrow."

"I come back on Monday, right?"

"No, this is the last day."

"I'll see you again tomorrow, won't I?"

It seemed as if she wasn't all there mentally. Anya told us Maxim was like that when he started coming to church. Without Christ, there's no hope in this world. Maxim turned into an excellent children's worker and planned to attend Bible college.

On Friday evening the campers sang and performed dramas at a closing program for parents. Many parents who came were not believers, so the camp provided a positive contact with many families.

Though the camp was a success, we didn't go to Ukraine to lead camps. Cory wanted to help the church reach out more but realized no growth would take place unless the church council bought into the vision. He had ideas of how he wanted to serve, but he wanted to work with the leaders, not against them.

At the next council meeting, Cory asked the brothers, "How can I best help you? Do you want the church to grow? And if so, what is the best way to go about it?"

They didn't have any answers for him in that meeting, nor at the next. The question, "Do you want the church to grow?" became sidetracked as they blamed each other for problems in the church.

Andre had vision. He read Ephesians 4:11-16, saying that the work of leaders is to train and release others in the church to do ministry. Some dismissed his comments as impractical.

"They don't realize that having a vision is half of the battle," Cory told me later. "Once the congregation owns it, it will take off. Right now, all they can see is more work for the brothers. They haven't learned the principle of equipping the saints for work of ministry."

The church council never did come up with a vision statement but eventually decided Cory could preach every week and work with Stefan.

Right before each church service, all the brothers—men in some leadership position—gathered in "the brothers' room." During the five or ten minute meeting, the pastor chose who would preach during the service. Each service contained three sermons. Though some ad-libbed, Cory learned to come prepared.

Cory tried to impart vision with his sermons. "It's not comfortable to reach out to people who are different," he told the congregation. "It wasn't comfortable for Peter to go to the Gentiles, but God wants all people to know Him."

Cory preached in Russian. It wasn't perfect, but the congregation understood him adequately. Sometimes though, especially during his first year of preaching, people laughed when it wasn't supposed to be funny. As time went on, he got the pronunciation down better.

One tricky word in Russian is "write" or "wrote," as in, "The apostle Paul wrote...." A similar word, with a different stress, is "urinate." When learning another language, one must be willing to make mistakes and sound like a fool.

Cory didn't want to depend on a translator. Translators weren't always available, and he felt he could connect with people better if he didn't go through another person. With this determination, he learned Russian. People respected his willingness to learn their language.

"Quite a few people told me we should immigrate and make Ukraine our home," Cory told me. "Not that we'd want to, but it shows that they accept us."

Cory got more language practice than I did, but I could go to the market and converse. Many people asked if I was from the Baltic region, because of my fair hair and skin, and they said I spoke Russian with a Baltic accent. I thought it was a great compliment until someone told me, "You sound Baltic; they speak bad Russian like you."

Cory and Stefan started looking for a car for us. Cory had been reluctant to buy a car right away because cars could be more of a hassle than a blessing. First we would need to rent a garage somewhere, since cars left on the street overnight became a source of free spare parts. Cory also wanted to have enough Russian to know what to do and say at the many police checks on the road, and he knew church members would call on him for taxi service.

We could reach most places in Feodosia within a thirty-minute walk. We learned how to ride the bus, which cut down on shoe wear but didn't always save time. Buses were often very crowded. If we wanted to go to another town, we had to call on Stefan or someone else with a car.

Cory told Stefan he wanted a newer Russian car so we wouldn't have to spend all our time fixing it. Stefan said that even if we bought a car straight from the factory, we would still have to fix it, since they don't put them together very well.

Stefan finally found a car for us in Kiev. Someone in Germany had sent a German-made Ford to a ministry in Kiev where Stefan's brother was the director. They didn't need it and wanted to sell it. That car was a gift from God.

We found a garage. It was a twenty-five-minute hike from our house, so we continued to walk and take the bus around town. It didn't make sense to get the car for trips to the market, since I could walk there in five minutes, but we needed it for travel to other towns and villages. Cory purchased fruit and vegetables along the road when he was out driving with Stefan, so the car did reduce my shopping load.

When my birthday rolled around, Cory upgraded our ancient four-foot refrigerator to a full-sized model. One year earlier, we had been stranded up on the hill with no oven, no cake, and no friends to help us celebrate. This was a good birthday, though. Cory and the girls baked a cake. Anya brought flowers. Alicia gave me her doll. "You can sleep with her," she offered.

Later that summer our parakeet, Malinki, died. After our initial shock of finding his lifeless body in the cage, Janelle gave a big sigh and said, "We need to give our problems to Jesus."

Alicia said, "Our birdie is in heaven now."

The girls skipped and hopped all the way to the market when I took them to pick out a new bird. The girls named him Christopher, short for Christopher Robin. Christopher was friendly and preferred to sit on someone's shoulder than in his cage.

Anya's cat had learned to run for his life when the girls came over. Without a cat to cuddle, Alicia adopted Christopher. He gladly rode on her shoulder but objected when she tried to stuff him in her purse.

The electricity was typically off for two hours in the morning and two hours in the evening. I could accept that, but sometimes we went without for much longer periods. Water was off several hours every day as a conservation measure, especially during the summer. I don't know why we had water outages after autumn rains began. (Probably because I wanted to do laundry and Big Brother was watching.)

I had just heated the wash water one day when the water stopped. I had none for rinsing but expected it to come on shortly. I proceeded to wash, piling soapy clothes in the tub. Running water didn't return until the next day. By then, the clothes had a sour smell, which didn't rinse out. I wrote in my journal:

> I don't mind water outages if I can plan around them. Turn the water off every day from nine to five, if you like. Just give me something I can count on!! In a world of uncertainty, I have renewed appreciation for the faithfulness of God. "Thou changest not; Thy compassions, they fail not. As Thou hast been, Thou forever will be."
>
> We have a book about women missionaries called, *Guardians of the Great Commission.* When I read about the hardships and dangers these women lived with—and often died from—my trials seem trivial.
>
> I sometimes wonder when I'll be so in love with God that I can freely say, "Your will, no matter what!" Life here has been more difficult than I expected. It's not enough to say, "Yes, God" only once. I need to continue with an attitude of willingness in the midst of unpleasant circumstances.

Life was even more difficult for the local people. Record-breaking heat and drought that summer damaged many crops. Our neighbor had planted a garden outside town to supplement her pension. Without water, it wilted, so she had to buy most of her produce at the market. The price of potatoes and flour doubled. Many dreaded the coming winter.

Tatiana said her husband finally received his April salary, not in money but in sugar and rice. "We'll be eating rice until we turn Chinese!" she said. Still, it was better to be paid in rice than in vodka, as some had.

She said her acquaintance who taught in a village had a son who also taught. In lieu of their salary, the two of them received 300 bottles of vodka. She didn't drink and didn't want to stand on a street corner trying to sell the stuff.

The most severe power outages took place during the peak of tourist season. This put tremendous hardship on cafes, restaurants, and anyone trying to serve visitors. Russian tourists brought money to town, but many said during this visit that they wouldn't return to Feodosia.

One man told us, "Old-timers say life is worse now than it was after World War II. Our whole town was destroyed in the war, but every month you could see some improvement. People are very pessimistic now because every month it just gets worse."

Ukraine's currency, the coupon, had dropped in value from 150,000 per American dollar when we arrived to 175,000 per dollar over the year. The government had printed a new bank note, the hryvna, to replace the coupon. They would simply move the decimal point over five places and make it 1.75 hryvna per dollar.

The announced currency change brought some panic to the streets and the exchange rate jumped to 205,000 coupons per dollar for several days as people tried to buy hard currency. The last time new bills had been introduced was when Ukraine gained independence from the Soviet Union.

Several people told us they had scrimped and saved money over many years during Soviet times. They kept it in the bank and had enough money to buy a new car. When they went to the bank after independence to withdraw their funds, they had only enough to buy a stick of sausage.

Some told us, "I'll never put money in the bank again." People usually hid their money around the house. If they had extra, they tried to buy U.S. dollars or hard goods, the only ways to save money in the face of rapid inflation and currency devaluation.

When the new currency change was announced, people lined up outside money exchange booths and banks trying to buy dollars. No bank was selling though, only buying. After several weeks, the exchange rate settled down again and the new bills became the only ones in circulation.

We felt overwhelmed by the many needs around us, both physical and spiritual. I read a quote which went something like this: "When you see a missionary coming home weary and broken, remember it's not the things he's done which sap the soul, but rather, the things he couldn't do."

I reminded myself, Jesus didn't try to meet all the needs around Him, yet He could still say in the end, "I've finished the work You gave me to do." We hoped we could say the same at the end of our term—but we didn't know what we should do or how we could make any difference.

One day I stood at the sink washing dishes under a trickle of water and listed reasons why I didn't like being a missionary in Ukraine. It was just a partial list, since it would take too long to review everything. Stress on the family. Cory hadn't found any fulfilling ministry. Separation from loved ones. Inconveniences. Unexpected outages of water and electricity. The sense of being out of control. I missed the "normal life" where you get what you earn.

The sound of the television interrupted my thoughts. The girls were watching a video, a gift from someone we had never met. It made me think of other blessings. Our new water filter was another gift, and it gave us clean drinking water that no longer tasted like swamp. Our monthly financial report recorded the generosity of so many. We were privileged to have daily prayer support. We did nothing to earn these gifts, and we had no way to repay.

Gifts of grace. Grace is something you don't earn—can't earn. It goes beyond salvation. We had health. Adequate food. A good car. We had friends who loved us, in Ukraine and abroad. Stefan gave us a gunnysack of potatoes and wouldn't accept payment. Anya earned just $40 a month but often bought treats for Janelle and Alicia. I felt humbled by their generosity.

"Normal" folks get what they earn. They have their feet squarely on the ground and feel some sense of control. Living by faith has me dangling from a parachute or a hot-air balloon—or something up there—no, Someone. The cord is strong and when I'm grateful, the view is fine.

I stood at the sink and listed my gifts of grace. Only a partial list, for it would take too long to list everything.

Many children attending camp came from non-Christian homes

Women from the church prepared lunch

- 14 -
Hope Endures

The local church had problems, but God still touched the lives of spiritually needy people. One Sunday morning early in October, I attended Janelle and Alicia's Sunday School class. One little girl stood out. While the other girls had long hair put up in braids and bows, this girl had very short hair, unwashed and poorly cut. There was something else different about her: her face glowed more than all the rest.

I hadn't met Lena when she came to church camp in July, but I'd heard about this timid child with filthy, infected hands. She was like a neglected plant without water or sunlight. With a little loving care, her hands healed and she blossomed. She began attending Sunday School after the camp.

I watched her recite her memory verse with enthusiasm and bask in praise. Anya told me, "Lena has never been to school even though she is already eight. Her parents are drunkards."

That morning, her mother came to church too, wearing ill-fitting pants and rouge on her tired face. She went forward to repent at the end of the service. I hoped she would feel enough love to blossom too.

Two teenage girls from the church came to visit us one day and send an e-mail message to Americans who helped with the camp. While Masha, age seventeen, hunted and pecked on the computer, I talked to fourteen-year-old Sveta.

Sveta's father had died the previous week after eating poisonous mushrooms. He had been drinking, which strengthens the toxic effects. While he lay in a coma, Sveta's mother called us to see if we had any medicine for poison. The hospital had none. We didn't either. He died two days later.

I read a news report afterward which said 92 people in Ukraine had died that year from mushroom poisoning with 1100 more hospitalized. With harsh economic conditions, many people went to the forest to gather free food.

Sveta told me, "God helps us and life goes on."

"How did you become a Christian," I asked.

Her twenty-year-old brother had accepted Christ in another city and encouraged her and her mother to go to church. She had been attending for one year. "At first, it was difficult," she said.

I assumed it was hard or her to be around legalistic old ladies but asked, "Why?"

"I came out of the world," she replied. "I was dirty inside. I knew the church was a good place to be, but at first when I tried to live as a Christian, I fell often. Jesus has lifted me up. He has made me clean inside. I feel lighter and life is easier now."

Masha had also been attending church for a little over one year. She, too, told us, "I knew I was a sinner and needed Jesus." I wrote about their comments in my journal and added:

> I thought about the group of American musicians who performed in Feodosia last year. Their testimonies all followed the line: "I wanted happiness so I tried this and that, but I wasn't happy until I tried Jesus." I never heard "I was a sinner and Jesus forgave my sin." Happiness is fleeting but hope endures.
>
> It seems most Americans think "pursuit of happiness" is the ultimate goal in life. After all, it's in our Constitution, so isn't it our divine right—especially if we are good Christians?
>
> While criticizing shallow-thinking Americans, I have to look in the mirror. I've had the notion if I obey God, I'll be truly fulfilled. Running the race isn't always fun or fulfilling. God blesses His children, but sometimes I have to hang in there as an act of endurance—not for the blessing, but because God deserves it.

Tatiana's two close friends moved away. She told us with tears in her eyes, "You aren't a friend in the Russian sense, but Victor and I are very fond of your family."

Americans speak of friends loosely. We have friends from school, friends at work, friends at church. Americans need only one good conversation to feel that they have a new friend, but for a Russian, it takes years.

The communist system drove distrust deep into the Russian soul. Russians use the word "acquaintance" in all but the most trusted of relationships. Many have no one they can call "friend."

We liked Tatiana and her husband Victor too. Sometimes he came to visit during our Russian lesson. While Tatiana tutored us, Victor entertained Janelle and Alicia by forming animals from clay.

Victor worked at two different places as a security guard. One day he had two 24-hour shifts back to back. He hurried home from one job, washed his face, grabbed something to eat, and headed off to his other job.

The timekeeper demanded to know why he was fifteen minutes late. Victor felt tired and angry but replied, "I haven't been paid since April so I haven't eaten since April. On my way to work I fainted from hunger, and it took me fifteen minutes to recover." The timekeeper laughed and let him go.

Tatiana started reading her Bible more. She told us Victor picked it up one day, opened it, and his eyes fell on the words, "Do not lay up for yourselves treasures on earth, where moth and rust destroy, and thieves break in and steal." He marveled at the truth of those words.

She told us, "Now that I'm reading the Bible, I'm surprised to see how many quotes attributed to Lenin actually came from the Bible. For example, our leaders often quoted Lenin as saying, 'He who is not for us is against us.' Of course we weren't allowed to read the Bible ourselves."

A music group from Kansas offered to come in October and hold an evangelistic music event in Feodosia. The church invited them and referred to the event as a "festival." Stefan and Cory worked on posters and handouts for advertising. Giorgi, the shoemaker, found a sound system and invited choirs from other churches in Ukraine. Tatiana, who had contacts all over the city, arranged for the Americans to perform in several schools.

Many posters were ripped down. The Orthodox church stepped up their campaign warning people not to turn to false religions, which meant any church other than the Orthodox church.

Cory preached on personal evangelism on the Sunday before the festival and encouraged the congregation to use the event as a way to introduce others to Christ. After his pep talk, he stood outside and gave away a stack of printed invitations to those who filed out.

The ladies' singing group arrived jet-lagged from Kansas. They had a busy schedule, but I enjoyed the time I had with them. When I heard them sing, I felt like crying the whole time. It was like I'd been on a starvation diet and their music fed my soul.

About 200 people came the first evening of the three-day music festival. I counted around 300 on the last day. Quite a few students and teachers came because of contacts made in schools. All who wanted one received a Russian New Testament.

The music group from Yalta, another city in Crimea, held an outdoor concert near the waterfront one evening. With superb weather, many people were out walking. Vitalik, a Russian evangelist from Yalta, and his fifteen-member music team set up loudspeakers around 7:00 and began to sing. Between songs, Vitalik spoke of the love and hope Jesus offers. Over one hundred people stopped, stayed, and listened.

A sidewalk cafe/bar nearby turned off its rock music so those patrons heard the Christian concert too. In the gathering dusk, this spot seemed the brightest in all of Feodosia.

Janelle had a cough and wanted to go home. I listened as far as the loudspeakers allowed while we walked away into the night. Cory later brought home the final report. The police came to investigate. Stefan and Cory took a couple Bibles over to the police car.

"Come closer so you can hear better," invited Stefan.

"We can hear fine from here," one officer said. They took the Bibles and left the team alone.

Vitalik invited the audience to come forward to pray and receive Bibles. Other than a few on the outskirts, the group stepped forward as one. Some wept. They passed out around 150 New Testaments. Grateful recipients carefully turned pages, holding the book up to a streetlight for a better look.

A drunken man approached Vitalik afterwards. "My wife and children were murdered, so today I killed one of the killers with these, my trembling hands. Perhaps this Bible will help me and keep me from killing someone again."

Many people came to the festival in the auditorium, but the outdoor concert brought the message of hope to those who wouldn't walk through doors to attend a religious meeting. In the following weeks, a few newcomers attended church services, but most never came back.

Cory got to know Andre better while the team was in town, since Andre provided transportation with his van. He told Cory, "We need to do more evangelism, and somehow we need to plant more churches."

Stefan also wanted to be involved with evangelism. He came by our house and poured out his frustrations. He said he didn't want to work with Igor any more but wasn't sure what to do. "It's good if two can work together," he said, "but it's impossible when one person constantly criticizes the other." He wanted to resign from the church council and find some kind of ministry on his own. "Or maybe I should just sit in the back and do nothing like other people."

Cory encouraged him to persevere a little longer.

Living conditions and our bad bed took a toll on my back. I hauled groceries from the market and wet laundry to the balcony. I carried water for heating and storage. Rinsing clothes in the tub strained my back, though kneeling helped.

One Sunday morning in early November, I leaned over to pick a paper off the floor and my back went out. I couldn't stand, sit, or walk without extreme pain. Cory carried me to bed while I screamed. Janelle and Alicia brought dolls and teddy bears to comfort me. Every time I yelped with pain, Janelle ran to her room to pray for me.

Cory canceled his plans for church and stayed home to take care of the girls and me. We e-mailed a doctor on our mission board and got his recommendation. We had brought various prescription drugs from the U.S. with us and had what we needed to ease the pain some. Still, recovery took a long time.

One advantage to the arrangement, I could lie in bed and read to my heart's content. I usually felt I had too much work to do to relax much. I wondered if I was addicted to work, too much like Martha who was "distracted by her much serving." I read the story again in Luke 10. I understood her position—she had thirteen hungry men to feed and no microwave or callout pizza. I would have been angry with Mary too.

I noticed Jesus didn't rebuke Martha for her effort but for her attitude. "Worried and bothered about too many things." I've never cooked for thirteen hungry men, but I grumbled at my load and I usually thought there was too much to do to sit around.

Could I sit at Jesus' feet and work at the same time? Brother Lawrence, author of *Practicing the Presence of God*, thought so. This monk didn't retreat to some cave to practice spirituality; he worshiped while working in a kitchen. People were so attracted to his Christ-like character they traveled many miles to talk with him while he peeled potatoes.

Tatiana came for our regularly scheduled Russian lesson and later returned with some instrument of torture, a sheet of plastic with plastic "needles" poking out of one side. She pressed that on my back several times, then applied heat-rub ointment. It helped some but brought no miracle relief.

Midweek, a nurse in our church who specializes in massage called on me. Built like a wrestler, she attacked my back with vigor, as though trying to scrub away a stubborn layer of skin. She applied heat-rub ointment, covered my bare back with wool and instructed me to stay in bed five more days. Five days!?! Cory was ready to do something besides wash dishes.

I asked her if Feodosia had chiropractic doctors. She said there was. She began learning the practice but stopped when her teacher paralyzed someone. I decided not to pursue that option.

She kindly came by the next day to beat me up some more. After working me over, she showed me her bag of medicine and said she wanted to give me an injection in the back.

I refused as nicely and forcefully as I could. Thanks, but no thanks. *Really,* it's not necessary. Your massage helped a lot. I'm feeling *much* better now.

Stefan and Nadia came by later to visit. They couldn't understand why I didn't want the injection. I had heard too much about dull Russian needles to want to try one first hand.

I read the book, *Christy,* about a sheltered nineteen-year-old girl who moved to the Appalachian Mountains to teach in a mission school. Culture shock set in. Appalled by the dirt, poverty, and strange customs, she said that maybe her parents were right and she didn't belong there.

The Quaker missionary told her she would never see the terrible side of life in sheltered ivory towers. Was she supposed to be there or was she just running away from home? Everyone has something good to contribute, but if she didn't do the work that was hers to do, it may never get done.

I didn't know what we'd ever contribute in Ukraine, but I wanted to persevere until God moved us on to something else.

- 15 -
We Battle Not Against Flesh and Blood

The church council suggested Cory could lead Bible studies for the young people. Most Bible study leaders lectured, using the same method followed in schools, where an authority told pupils what to think and believe.

Cory encouraged discussion as he worked through the Gospel of John. "What do you think this verse means?" he asked. "How does it apply to your life?" Most were reluctant to offer their thoughts, but some eventually warmed up. Cory examined verses in context and compared them with similar verses.

He also met weekly with twenty-year-old Sasha, a new believer, to train him as a co-leader. A few days before the group Bible study, Cory covered the chapter with him and gave him suggestions on how to help lead the discussion. Sasha often said, "I can't believe how much I learn from you."

Leading a Bible study was fine, but Cory wanted to do more. He thought the church could maintain their own programs without American help, and he wanted to see people outside the church come to Christ.

"I would still like to see some evangelistic small groups started that focus on reaching non-believers," Cory told me, "but Igor says the church isn't ready for that. True, some members are not, but I know many people are. I've talked to several who want to minister but have no outlet."

Cory visited Igor to ask him again about his evangelistic goals. "If the church doesn't want to do evangelism in Feodosia," Cory said, "then I will focus my efforts elsewhere."

Igor replied, "You don't need to work elsewhere, since there are many people here who don't know Christ. Whatever you do, though, I don't want you to work with Stefan." He detailed how Stefan was dishonest, unreliable, and there was no hope he would ever change. We knew he had told other people the same things.

In our experience, however, Stefan showed great love for God and people through many acts of service. He had done much to help our family. Whenever Janelle and Alicia saw him, they shouted out his name and ran to him for a hug. Many people liked Stefan, and we concluded that Igor felt threatened by his popularity.

We didn't think we could or should cut off our relationship with Stefan. When he came to our home that week, he spoke about his strained relationship with Igor. He felt grieved and wasn't sure what to do.

I said, "It would be easy to get bitter about the things Igor says, but please forgive him."

"I have forgiven him," Stefan said. "I hold nothing against Igor. The KGB used to raid my house every year looking for unauthorized Christian literature, at least that was their excuse. They threw everything to the floor and made a big mess. The last time, they took me to their car and I thought I would never see my wife and children again. Still, I forgave them. Satan had blinded their eyes from seeing the truth."

"But Igor is a believer," I said.

"Sin blinds the eyes of believers too. I can't hold anything against him."

I felt humbled, like I was sitting with a spiritual giant. Who was I to instruct him on forgiveness?

Stefan stayed and talked for five hours. He said the brothers were tired of being run over by Igor, but it wasn't possible to dismiss the pastor, except perhaps for some big sin.

A delegation went to Stefan's house pleading, "Please ask Cory to help us start a new church." Anya periodically begged Cory, "Please help Andre start a new church in Feodosia."

Men on the church council discussed the idea of a new church but decided it would have a rough start without Igor's blessing and knew a church split would result in hard feelings.

Cory thought it was pointless to found a church based on discontentment. People starting a new church need to have a bigger goal than "to get away from people we don't like." It's of no value to pour new wine into an old wineskin. He thought church plants should grow out of evangelistic Bible studies for nonbelievers.

At the next church council meeting, Cory again brought up the question, "What is the church going to do about evangelism?"

One council member said, "Our problem is that we think of evangelism only in terms of inviting people to church services. I have invited people, but non-Christians don't feel comfortable in our church. I think we should start a new church." Several agreed, but Igor wasn't ready for that.

Cory suggested starting evangelistic Bible studies in homes. Some expressed interest, but Igor said no.

Stefan said he wanted to resign from the church council but the other brothers wouldn't let him. They said he should remain on the council, but he wouldn't have to work with Igor any more. They decided Stefan and Cory should evangelize together in the nearby village of Vladeslovovka.

"I feel like I'm walking a tight rope," Cory said when he got home. "I really don't want to get involved in church politics; I just want to encourage them to reach people outside the church. Igor has no plan for evangelism, but when someone else does, it's threatening to him. He's afraid of losing control. Sometimes I wonder if the problems are all my fault, but people tell me the problems existed before we got here."

Vladeslovovka was a village near Feodosia with about 10,000 people. It had no church, not even an Orthodox church, and Stefan wanted to try to plant one there. He thought they could start by showing the *Jesus* film. He talked to the director of the Cultural Hall who agreed to let him use the auditorium for showing the film.

Cory and Stefan drove to Vladeslovovka to hang up posters advertising the film. A woman informed them that the village had absolutely no electricity, and they didn't expect any until after the first of the year. The collective farm that supported the village had shut down for the winter, and all services to the village had been stopped. Without electricity, they couldn't run the film projector. Disappointed, they took the posters down—maybe next year.

Then we heard that the Orthodox Church in Feodosia printed 3000 brochures warning people to stay away from the Baptist church and the foreigners they brought to town. I got a copy of this brochure from Luba. Her children got one at school, where teachers had passed them out.

The article had many big words, so I sat down with my Russian-English dictionary to find out what was so bad about the Baptist church and foreign missionaries. The brochure was titled, "What the Orthodox Church says about the erroneous sect Baptists." It began by quoting Matthew 7:15—beware of false prophets who come in sheep's clothing but are really ravenous wolves.

"What has happened in our Holy Russia? From far countries, from across enemy seas, an unclean horde has been rushing upon us to make war against holy believers and against the Orthodox Church."

It went on to describe how the Baptist church ignores apostolic tradition and distorts the Word of God since they don't baptize infants, they don't kneel before icons, and they believe salvation is a free gift of God.

It ended with, "Preserve your holy faith in the Orthodox church. For without her, no one will receive salvation. Jesus created one church, not many. This means there is salvation through only one faith and one church: Orthodox. If you accept Baptist fables and take their baptism, then you will excommunicate yourself from the Orthodox church and will destroy your soul forever."

Tatiana told us of a news report she saw on television. They showed footage of open graves in the Simferopol cemetery and said that foreign missionaries were to blame for the spread of Satan worship. The report quoted government authorities as saying they need tighter controls on giving visas to foreigners. "Though not all encourage Satan worship, they cause conflict with our own churches."

When we talked to Stefan about the news report and brochure, he said, "This is nothing compared to what we faced during the 70s. They accused Baptists of terrible things. They took our children from us."

Still, it felt strange to us to be called "the enemy." We are nice people. I had always skimmed over Jesus' words, "Don't be surprised when people hate you" since I never experienced it before.

Few people on the street knew we were Americans or foreigners since we looked like everyone else. Nevertheless, I felt even less inclined to want to tell anyone I was an American working with the local Baptist church. I understood a little bit better why the Russian Baptists isolated themselves and felt timid about sharing their faith.

Regarding the spread of Satan worship, I suppose some imported music didn't help, but Russians had occult activity long before foreigners were allowed in the country. Psychic healers were plentiful. Many trusted in the horoscope.

I found an article in the *Kiev Post* describing the popular use of witchcraft. "Hard Times a Blessing for Ukraine's Many Witches," read the headline. It said that many people in Ukraine visit soothsayers, witches, and healers in order to obtain good luck in business, to remove a curse, or place a curse.

A psychic healer interviewed claimed the practice of witchcraft in Ukraine was just as common as the practice of religion. She said her work centered on healing, but she knew how to cast a curse—it was common knowledge, inherited from older generations in the villages.

Besides those who took individual clients, some held mass séances. One popular healer claimed her grandmother treated Tsar Nicholas before the revolution. Admission was free to her ninety-minute séance, but vendors sold her photo and talismans that supposedly held powers from a spell she had cast on them. She placed an icon on the stage and said she gave excess money to churches.

I asked Tatiana what Ukrainian people believe about Satan. "Village people believe in many devils," she said. There are spirits that live in the stable and look after the animals. If you want to have healthy animals, you need to do something special to keep the stable spirits happy.

There are spirits who live in the water. Some say if you look into the water, they will pull you in. During a full moon, young maidens who have drowned come up, dance on the shore and sing beautiful songs to try to entice and drown young men.

Village homes have big ovens in the middle for cooking, for warmth and for the family to sleep on. These ovens have spirits too—people talk to them and give them gifts of food.

"The most awful beliefs have to do with the dead," she said. After a funeral, the relatives sit together in one room for three days so they can keep the surviving family members from opening the door at night. If someone opens the door, the dead person will bite him on the neck and turn him into a vampire. That vampire will bite other relatives and turn them into vampires. There were tales of whole villages of vampires.

Ukrainian fairy tales are often gruesome—not good reading for bedtime stories. When one teen came to visit and play with the girls, she always wanted to pretend she was a witch who ate children. She couldn't understand why I wanted her to play something more pleasant.

Some think adversity and the presence of adversaries means the door is closed. Paul, however, wrote to the Corinthians, "a wide door of effective service has been opened to me, and there are many adversaries." One can have fruitful ministry in spite of opposition.

Since Cory and Stefan couldn't start anything in Vladeslovovka, they decided to help the weaker churches. They started in Batalnaya, a village where the Primorski church had started a new church.

Cory and Stefan planned to show the *Jesus* film twice in Batalnaya: once at the church and then at the House of Culture as an outreach to the community.

About thirty-five people gathered for the first showing. There wasn't a dry eye before the film finished. The following week, they took the film to the House of Culture, an auditorium once used to propagate the gospel of Communism.

This particular auditorium was very cold that December day. Since the weather had turned nasty, only thirty people showed up. Wind blew through broken windows, chilling Cory to the bone, but everyone who came stayed until the end.

Fortunately, our apartment was warmer than the previous winter, since Cory bought a propane heater and installed foam weather-seal around windows and doors. We still wore long underwear, but I wasn't cold all the time. Having learned from the last year's frozen potatoes, he also moved our potatoes and apples off the balcony and tucked them under Alicia's bed.

Cory helped plan a Christmas party for teens from our church and several other churches. I made 140 popcorn balls, as a unique treat for the youth, friends, and neighbors. When Alicia started throwing up around 3:00 a.m., I knew she had found the popcorn balls.

The girls attended a New Year's party at church. While they sang and played games with other children, Cory and Igor talked.

You took Stefan away from me," Igor said. "Who will help me now?"

"The brothers decided," Cory replied.

"You just want to take over as pastor."

Cory was shocked. "I don't want to be pastor. I want to support you and your goals but I don't know what they are. The brothers don't know what your goals are. It's hard for people to follow you if they don't know where you are going."

"If I told them my goals they wouldn't support me. People follow you just because of money." He again accused Stefan of being untrustworthy. His charge went against everything we had seen in Stefan.

Stefan and Cory continued to show the *Jesus* film in various locations. During their many trips together, Cory pieced together Stefan's story.

In a village one hundred kilometers south of Kiev, lived a Christian man. People in his village ridiculed him for his faith—until World War II. Every time there was a bomb attack, everyone gathered at this man's house where he would read the Bible and pray. His house was the only one that never got hit or hurt. Everyone in the village of around two hundred people became Christians and Stefan's father was one of them.

Military service in any country is difficult, but believers faced more difficulty under communist leaders. Along with all other eighteen-year-old boys, Stefan went into the service. Of the 8,000 men on his base, he was the only Christian—the only one who stood up for his beliefs, anyway.

Stefan obeyed his leaders, except he refused to take the oath of loyalty to Communism since it required him to denounce belief in God. Night after night, superiors roused him from his bed and forced him to stand at attention. They interrogated him for hours, mocked him, and encouraged him to give up his foolish beliefs.

Two weeks of sleepless nights took its toll. He became very tired, very discouraged, and didn't know how much longer he could go on.

While Stefan was working alone one day, a man with broad shoulders, dressed in uniform came up to him and called him by name. He encouraged Stefan not to give up. "Hang on to your faith," he said. "It's difficult now, but they will respect you."

Stefan had never seen the man before and never saw him again. Could it have been an angel? Stefan felt strengthened and the interrogations soon ceased.

One day the commanding officer called Stefan into his office and sent him alone on a mission. He traveled two days by train to deliver a letter to another military office. The letter instructed the office to give Stefan a large amount of money to take back to the army base. The official who received the letter was surprised that Stefan was traveling alone and had no gun, but guns weren't issued to Christians.

When Stefan delivered the bag of money still sealed, his commanding officer told him, "What I've been told all my life about you Baptists isn't true. You are the most trustworthy person I know. Do you have a Bible I could read?" The officer gave Stefan a three-day freedom pass to go anywhere. "Just don't tell anyone," he said.

After Stefan completed his military service, he was warmly welcomed home—especially by the girls. Nice Christian boys are always in short supply. Stefan made the mistake once of walking a girl home from church. The girl's mother insisted that Stefan should marry the girl.

Stefan wasn't ready for marriage and wasn't about to let some desperate mother push him into it. Nor was he ready for all the attention he received from the other girls at church. The harsh atmosphere of military life and lack of Christian fellowship left him feeling dry and he wanted to get back on his feet spiritually. The mother told the church council that Stefan was trifling with her daughter's affections but wouldn't marry her. The council called him in for an explanation.

In Ukraine, singles don't date around, at least not in the church culture. If a guy sees a girl at church who might make a good wife, he tells her he would like to get to know her better. If the girl thinks he would make good husband, she agrees to spend time with him. If all goes well, they usually marry within a year. Walking a girl home, however, does not signify engagement.

Stefan explained his side the best he could, but the mother persisted in her attempt to catch him as her son-in-law. He decided to leave his village and move to Feodosia, where his older brother lived.

In Feodosia he wouldn't socialize with the girls he met at church. If a girl asked him to walk her home, he refused. "If you don't want to walk in the dark, you'd better leave early," he said. He wasn't about to get trapped again.

There was one girl in the church from a village not far from Stefan's hometown. Though they already knew each other, they rarely talked. Nadia admired Stefan from a distance but had little hope for any future together. As she was leaving one day for a two-week visit to see her family, Stefan went to the train station to see her off.

"I'd like to marry you," he said, "but I want you to think about it while you're gone." They married a few months later, much to the surprise of everyone in the church.

Stefan worked at the optics factory for many years. Among other things, the factory made lenses for night scopes and other military equipment. Stefan worked in the military section until the KGB discovered he was a Christian. They forced him to transfer to a different department, even though he was the best worker and his boss liked him. Since Christians were "enemies of the State," they couldn't have a Christian working around military secrets.

The KGB started harassing Stefan even more after his wedding, since his wedding party sang Christian songs in public. They raided his house and assigned someone to sit next to him at work to watch him all day, every day. Stefan talked to the man about his faith. After one year of this, the man suddenly became paralyzed and within one day, died.

A KGB agent told Stefan, "You prayed to your God and he did this." Supposedly, Communists don't believe in God, but they left him alone at work after that.

- 16 -
Our Tiny Flame

Andre wanted to encourage churches in the region to become intentional in their evangelistic efforts. Using his position as overseer for the churches of Eastern Crimea, he called a January meeting for the leaders of these churches. He invited Cory to attend as well.

Around thirty-five leaders from seven churches attended the meeting. Andre began by reading the Great Commission passage from Matthew 28. Then he read the verses in Ephesians 4, which discuss the need to equip people for ministry for the building up of the body of Christ.

He divided everyone into groups by church and asked them to discuss and write answers to the following questions: What can your church start doing now to reach the world and reach your community? How can you equip people for ministry? What do you need to reach these goals?

Afterward participants shared their thoughts about Andre's questions. One old man stood up and talked a long time on the importance of preserving traditions. The majority, however, showed openness to new ideas.

Andre planned to hold a second seminar for church leaders in February. He told Cory later, "I was a little deceptive during the first meeting, since I never told them what my goal is."

Cory agreed with his approach, "You have to make people feel a need before they want to meet the need."

The following week, the weather warmed up enough for me to take the girls for a walk. Near the sea, we ran into Mikhail, a believer in his 30s. He taught school in a village, but their classrooms lacked heat, so they had an extended holiday until the end of January.

"Thank you for the fish you sent us," I said. "How did you like Andre's seminar?"

He said he thought the seminar was great, but it left him with questions. How *do* you reach the world for Christ? How do you equip others for ministry? He thought he needed to be better equipped himself.

"I've known the Lord only two-and-a-half years," he said. "I was so excited when I heard the Gospel. It seemed like such a miracle that Christ died for me. Of course, I wanted to live for Him and I told many people about Him, but everyone was skeptical. I couldn't understand why they didn't want to know Christ too. Now I see they are in the grasp of Satan and I need to pray more."

Mikhail had accepted Christ when an American visited their town and held evangelistic meetings. The American baptized him and a teenage girl.

After the American left, the "senior brother" in the church said the baptism was invalid. He discredited the American's message and called the baptism a "circus sideshow." A pastor from a neighboring village finally settled the dispute and judged that the baptism was indeed valid.

"I don't know how to preach," Mikhail said. "I've known the Lord only a short time." He said the Bible reading schedule Cory gave him helped him read his Bible more systematically.

"Our church is mostly old women," he continued. "They are going to die soon. How can we reach new people?" He was doing what he could. At Christmas, for example, he took the youth group caroling and evangelizing around town.

On our way home from feeding the swans another day, a man in dirty, shabby clothes fell in step with the girls and me. He smelled of alcohol. He said the girls were cute and asked if they were mine.

I nodded, not wanting to encourage conversation but not wanting to be rude, either.

"You married?" he asked.

"Yes," I said. "I have a good husband."

He invited me home with him.

I shook my head. "No, I cannot."

He blocked my path and grabbed my arm. I tried to pull away, but his grip was too strong. He threatened to beat me up if I didn't come with him. The girls began to cry.

I asked passersby to help, but they ignored me. Some crossed the street to avoid walking near us. I wondered if I should kick him, but decided against it and prayed instead. Then something distracted the man and he let go. I grabbed the girls, ran across the street, and ducked into a store. I felt shaken by the experience, by the feeling of helplessness, by the fact that no one would help me.

When we finally went home, the girls said they wanted to go far away to Oregon where that bad man wouldn't find us. The same thought occurred to me. Nevertheless, I suggested we pray for the man, forgive him, and thank God for keeping us safe.

Tatiana told me later that a similar event once happened to her. She also felt disturbed by the indifference of those passing by. She explained, "People think, 'That person probably did something to deserve it' and they don't want to cause problems for themselves by getting involved."

She recommended that I learn to say, "Leave me. My husband is a jealous man and he is waiting for me down the road. You will have problems if he sees you."

Janelle and Alicia didn't want to go for a walk the next day, nor the next. They were nervous about venturing outside for church on Sunday but decided if that bad man bothered them, Daddy would beat him up. Still, Cory had to carry Alicia most of the way to church.

When the director of School Number Two learned that real, live Americans lived in Feodosia, she wanted to meet us. This school, not far from our apartment, had a special English program. Cory was busy, but I called for an appointment. I thought I'd meet with her for ten or twenty minutes and be on my way. However, the director and head English teacher served coffee and cream pastries and kept me an hour and a half.

Their first question was, "What is your education?" They seemed pleased to learn I had a university degree. Communist propaganda portrayed Christians as uneducated and backwards.

I told them we would have college interns coming to spend two months in Feodosia that summer. Could they meet with English-speaking students?

The director thought an "English Club" would provide a wonderful opportunity for her students. She said a leader in the Orthodox church had rebuked her for allowing foreign Christians to speak at the school. Her response had been, "We have a special school and our students need exposure to native English speakers." Still, she told me the interns could discuss American culture at the English Club, but not the Bible.

Svetlanda, the teacher, urged me to come and talk to her classes. She was a no-nonsense woman who had been teaching English for years—

maybe centuries. She obviously loved her subject and expected her students to love it too. Who was I to refuse her request?

She met me at the school entrance the next day and steered me to a waiting group of students. I talked about myself and Oregon and students asked questions. They wanted to know why we came to Ukraine. When I told them we worked with the Baptist church, a hush fell over the group and they looked at each other, as though I had just said I was a Moonie—or a Martian.

I passed out American pennies. "All our money has 'In God We Trust' written on it," I said. "Many Americans now go by the motto 'In Money We Trust,' but faith in God was what made America strong. Ukraine will become strong only when it has a good moral base. Right now, foreign companies are afraid to invest in Ukraine because of corruption."

I glanced at Svetlanda, standing in a back corner, and saw her nod slightly.

The students asked many questions: Do you like Michael Jackson? What are your hobbies? Who is your favorite movie star? What kind of music do you like?

I said one reason I don't like popular rock songs is because of lyrics about violence and sex which don't show respect for other people. If someone says, "I want your body," it's lust, not love. Real love wants the best for the other person. Lust uses other people. A girl in the back row looked like she was about to cry.

I worried that Svetlanda might be offended that I preached to her students, but she pressed me to stay and talk to another class.

Separation from family was more difficult than coping with the living conditions. We came to Ukraine understanding we wouldn't see family again until the end of our four-year term. E-mail contact was wonderful, but little girls grow a lot in four years. I felt awful every time Janelle and Alicia asked to visit their cousins and every time I thought of them growing up without Grandma and Grandpa.

We asked our mission organization if we could take a short furlough mid-term, and they agreed. Since summer months would be busy with camps and American visitors, we planned to go home from mid-February until mid-May.

Janelle and Alicia responded to the news of our upcoming trip with an excited cheer. From the time they learned we would be in Oregon for Janelle's birthday, they prayed at every single meal, "And help us go to Aunt Linda's house and eat a birthday there."

We had been in Ukraine almost nineteen months when we left. As soon as I got on the airplane, I noticed how the flight attendants smiled at us. They even looked us in the eye. It made me cry to be treated kindly, like I was human.

In Ukraine, people rarely looked strangers in the face, certainly not in the eye. We learned to navigate crowded sidewalks by radar. Smiles were hard to find even in church, since many thought it's more spiritual to wear a solemn face.

As our airplane lifted off, I felt as if I had escaped from prison.

After our arrival, many people asked, "So, how do you like it over there?"

It's a normal question. I thought a well-adjusted missionary should be able to say, "Oh, I've never felt so fulfilled in all my life." Or at least, "It's rewarding, in spite of the difficulties."

I could only reply, "It's a difficult place to live, but that's where we feel God wants us for now." I decided that wasn't a lesser answer.

How did Moses like leading the Israelites? Did Paul enjoy getting beat up and shipwrecked? If you had asked Jesus, "So, how do you like living on earth?" what would He have said?

They all had a mission to accomplish. It would have been easier for Jesus to stay in heaven, "but for the joy set before Him, He endured the cross."

Likewise, in Hebrews 11, the "faith chapter," men and women chose to do difficult things, not for immediate reward, but in faith that something good would result.

I enjoyed many things about our furlough: hot water, washing machines, well-stocked stores, friendly clerks, and shopping carts. I could wear makeup to church without wondering if I would offend anyone. I liked being with family—watching the girls play with cousins and hug grandparents.

On my parents' farm, Alicia said on our walk through pine trees, "Grandpa got us *all* these pinecones to kick!"

We felt loved and supported when we visited various churches. While driving home one day, Cory said, "I feel like we are richer than most people I know…I mean in terms of relationships, friendships with people who care about us. We are really blessed."

We enjoyed church services in our heart language and felt as though we hadn't worshiped for almost two years. One sermon, however, put worship in another context. The pastor quoted King David's words, "I will not offer to God something which costs me nothing." Sacrifice is an act of worship.

I realized worship isn't simply meaningful songs, inspiring sermons, and close fellowship. Worship includes, "Jesus, I do this for you as an act of love and out of appreciation for your supreme sacrifice for me." Unfortunately, I usually focus on the cost more than Christ.

The girls liked being in the U.S. but after a couple months, they said they wanted to go to their "other house." When asked what she liked best about Ukraine, Janelle said, "My bed." We had been on the move a lot.

I prepared for our return to Ukraine with the enthusiasm of an escaped convict turning himself in. I knew God wasn't done with us in Ukraine and He had given us good friends there, but it was a difficult place to live.

What made life in Ukraine difficult? The living conditions were something like fifty or sixty years behind the U.S. Outhouses outnumbered microwaves by far. People tended gardens and canned produce in order to have fruit on hand during winter months. Women washed clothes by hand or used primitive washing machines.

I could live without a microwave and I liked to can. More difficult than the backwards living conditions was the pervasive sense of despair.

In the U.S. fifty or sixty years ago, life was constantly improving. The standard of living for most people in Ukraine, however, had gone down and they saw little hope for improvement.

Sure, there were wealthy people in Ukraine—Feodosia's streets held numerous BMW's. At the wedding of one mafia member the previous summer, a helicopter dropped flower petals on the newlyweds, and guests rode in a long line of limousines. Most residents, however, wondered when they would receive their next paycheck.

As an American in Ukraine, I could feed my family meat every day. I could afford to heat our apartment during the winter. I lived surrounded, though, by people whose eyes were clouded with a sense of despair.

God sees. He hears. He sent his Son so that people in darkness might see a great light. He sent us too. It was easier to live in the U.S., but the people of Ukraine had less opportunity to hear about this God of love. Those with less hope and less light needed our tiny flame the most.

-17-
"Always Ready"

Our second trip into Ukraine wasn't as intimidating as our first. At the airport in Kiev, we could understand announcements over the loudspeaker and could talk to the customs agent. We had a joyful reunion with Stefan, who met us at the airport.

He talked about the past three months during our long train ride to Crimea. He now led a Saturday evening service in the village of Batalnaya. His eyes glowed as he spoke about the new congregation there.

"There aren't enough brothers to preach the usual three sermons," he said, "so I give a short message and spend much of the time answering questions." Most attending were either new believers or seekers and Stefan found their thirst for spiritual truth refreshing.

He asked Cory, "Remember the director of the night club who said she didn't like the *Jesus* film? She has repented and now comes to church."

Arriving in Feodosia, we learned the water would be off for two days. Welcome home. Fortunately, the woman who stayed in our apartment stored some for us so we could wash. She also made us a pot of cabbage borscht. Our parakeet, Christopher, chirped a happy greeting.

Anya welcomed us warmly too and gave us a long update on her life. Right before we left, the church had held a member's meeting. They said that some Sunday School teachers wore makeup and therefore set a bad example for the children. Anya felt the concerns were directed at her. In the following weeks, some leaders had "talks" with her.

She struggled with their rebuke but finally concluded that God looked at her heart and that before Him, it wasn't a sin to wear makeup. "So now I wear makeup to church without fear" she told me. "I stopped wearing head-covering too, since I'm not married."

Andre had conducted another seminar for church leaders of Eastern Crimea during our absence. He focused on the need to use the Bible as our standard for truth. "Many people substitute traditions for God's word," he said. "They depend on people's opinions or rely on what they were told by grandma."

Stefan told us the message was well received, even though it was a new type of teaching. Preachers more often said, "Obey your leaders" (and their interpretation of the Bible) instead of encouraging people to look to the Bible as their standard.

Andre told Cory he saw a need for new churches. "The old ones are simply not able to grow," he said. Younger church leaders attending Andre's seminars wanted to do more outreach. Andre and Cory decided to meet with Stefan and come up with a strategy for training men such as these to plant new churches.

I brought back baby clothes for Tatiana and eagerly listened to an update on her pregnancy—she was due in August. In December, she had quizzed me about my pregnancies, before she was even sure it was the real thing.

The previous year, Tatiana often joined us for dinner after her work and before our language lesson. Cory had been bold enough to pray God would give her a child. I squirmed a bit. I knew she wanted a child, but she was already forty-two and had been married five years. Yet God heard and answered.

That spring Tatiana begged, "I want you to teach me what you know about breathing during delivery, the things they taught you in America." Like American women, Russian women tell labor horror stories—but their stories sound more terrible.

In Ukraine, Tatiana explained, they leave you alone in a room to go through labor on your own. If you haven't had your baby by the time the doctor wants to sleep at night, they inject you with a drug to make the contractions stop—then jump-start you again in the morning with a different drug. Some women went two or three days like that.

Tatiana expected shocked reactions from co-workers and acquaintances, especially because of her age. Conformity was important in Soviet culture and people scorned anything out of the ordinary. "When my sister had her first child at the age of twenty-five," she said, "the doctors scolded her. They told her, 'You are too old to have your first child. Why did you give us and yourself such a hard time by waiting so long?'"

Fortunately, Tatiana found most people supportive.

"Does Cory have any new strategies for evangelization?" Tatiana asked. It seemed like a strange inquiry from someone who had not yet "converted," but this wasn't the first time she had shown an interest in our success.

We discussed our summer plans and said we would need a translator for visitors. Two college students and a group from Kansas planned to come. "Will you be available?" I asked.

"I would like very much to help," she began. "It's not just for the money." Her eyes filled with tears. She took several moments to collect herself before she continued. "I see people in the street with so many needs. I don't know what I can do to help them, but I can help you. It's the least I can do."

Anya joined the girls and me for an outing in our courtyard. We talked while Janelle and Alicia climbed on rusty monkey bars. "In America, do you celebrate Jesus' ascension into heaven?" she asked. She had just returned from a church service honoring this event.

"No, we celebrate just Christmas and Easter," I replied. Russians have many more religious holidays. Besides Christmas and Easter, they honor Jesus' baptism, the transfiguration, the ascension, the day of Pentecost, and the day Mary learned she would have a child.

Anya said that even though she grew up in a nonreligious home in communist Russia, they still celebrated religious holidays. On the day of Pentecost, for example, they gathered flowers outside town. They decorated their house with flowers and vine garlands and sprinkled lemongrass on their floor.

"Mmm. It smelled so good," she recalled. "We never went to church, and I don't know why we decorated our house but it was fun. Maybe it was some pagan custom."

Anya pulled seed stalks from the tall grass and began to braid them together. With each twist, she added more stalks. Janelle and Alicia helped her gather grass stems. As she braided, she talked about her childhood.

Along with the other children in her first grade class, Anya was inducted into the "Octoberists," a club named after the October revolution. In a solemn ceremony, older children gave first graders red metal pins that pictured Lenin as a child.

Teachers diligently prepared students for the next level, Pioneer Club. To belong to Pioneers, you had to be a good student, obey your teachers and parents, help the elderly, and collect paper for recycling. All but the most naughty children joined Pioneers when they turned ten.

"I remember feeling so proud when they gave me my red scarf," Anya said. "The problem with schools these days is that they have no clubs which help build self esteem."

Leaders told them the red in the scarf was like a little piece of their flag. Red in the flag stood for the blood of those who died in the October revolution. "You too must be ready to give your life for your country."

All children learned the story of young Pavel Morozov. After the revolution, communist leaders required all citizens to give their cattle and land to state cooperatives. One "rich and greedy" man didn't want to share with others, so his son, Pavel Morozov, reported him to the authorities. The father was arrested. Pavel's uncle and brother took little Pavel to a field and beat him until he died. What a hero.

"We should be brave like Pavel and do what is right for our country," children were told.

When Pioneer Club rallies were held at the statue of Lenin, the leader would say, "Are you ready to fight for the Communist party?"

The young Pioneers saluted with right arms raised at a slant over their heads. "Always ready!" they replied in unison. Anya said the salute signified readiness from the top of the head to the bottom of their feet.

Communists banned Bibles and came up with their own book of moral instruction. "For example, 'He who does not work should not eat,' I just read that in the Bible yesterday," Anya said. "I didn't know it came from the Bible."

Schoolteachers told students, "There is no God. Religion is the opiate of the people. Christians are enemies of the state. Church is for foolish old women who don't know it has been scientifically proven no God exists—after all, our astronauts didn't see any old man sitting on the clouds. If you *do* go in a church, we will take away your red scarf and you can't belong to the Pioneers."

Young Pioneers prepared for the next step, which was to join Comsomol, an abbreviation for Communist Youth Union. Again, they were told to be good students, obey their leaders, and help others. They recycled glass and metal.

In preparation for joining Comsomol, they memorized facts about communism—for example: how many socialistic countries are there in the world? The right answer was that half the world was socialist, including many African countries, many Asian countries, and Cuba. They sang songs about how much they loved Cuba. They learned the whole world would soon be socialist since capitalism would fall.

They learned that in the United States, a few very wealthy people controlled the power while others were very poor and lived on the street and ate from garbage bins. It wasn't like in the USSR, where everyone shared and worked together.

Young people from Africa, Asia, and Cuba were brought to special Young Pioneer camps; one was in Crimea. The camps for foreigners were much nicer than the camps local children attended.

A young person could join Comsomol at the age of fourteen, after passing a quiz at the communist headquarters in town. Only members of Comsomol could obtain higher education. Since Christians would not or could not join Comsomol, they could not attend college or university. This prohibition reinforced propaganda that said Christians are ignorant and uneducated.

As a schoolteacher, Anya and the other teachers were invited to join the Communist Party—the final step. "I thought you had to have very high morals to be a Communist," she said. "I had been with men. I didn't think I was good enough to join the party."

When perestroika exposed how things really were within the party, she was glad she hadn't joined. Modern movies portrayed communist leaders as immoral and crooked.

She tied her braid in a circle using more grass stems and placed the fuzzy crown on Alicia's head. "Janelle, I'll make one for you too," she said. I helped the girls pull more stalks.

She began to braid again and said, "God worked a great miracle in my life when I became a Christian." All her life she had been taught it was foolish to believe in God. When she wrote on the assigned topic: "Why I don't believe in God," she received top marks.

"How *did* you become a Christian?" I asked.

When she faced many personal problems early in 1992, Anya sought help through the Orthodox Church. "I didn't really believe in God," she said, "just some kind of greater power."

The priest baptized her by using oil to make the sign of the cross on her forehead and hands. He required no statement of faith, just money.

"I got baptized," she said, "because I thought Saint Nicholas might help me more if I were baptized." Saint Nicholas was considered the saint of miracles and she prayed to his icon.

"I went to the Orthodox church services," Anya said, "but I didn't understand anything." The Bible readings and songs sung by the choir were in an ancient Slavic language. "I didn't know it was bad to drink, because even the priest got drunk."

Several months later, she saw a poster near the bread kiosk announcing a Christian music program, sponsored by the local Baptist church. She went. The songs and sermon touched her heart, so she went forward at the invitation to pray. She cried and cried as she confessed her sins—and finally felt the freedom of forgiveness.

For the next year, she attended a Bible study led by one of the brothers. Eight started out in the study, but only Anya ended up joining the church. She was baptized in the Black Sea at the end of that year-long study.

Anya said later, "I've seen another miracle too. That was when an American came from so far away to live here and she became my friend."

Caps of braided grass stalks

- 18 -
Our Second Summer

Cory brought two summer interns, American college students, to our house for dinner and orientation. They would live with local families, but spent the first night with us so we could get better acquainted.

The guy, age twenty-five, hoped to eventually work with Muslims and had gone on several mission trips before. As a teenager, he had lived in the woods for three months doing a survival camp and ate worms, bugs, and wild plants. His trip to Ukraine offered another fine adventure.

The girl, age nineteen, wanted to try mission work during her summer vacation but could hardly stop crying. She didn't use the dirty toilet on the train and the alternative seemed even more appalling. During the final two-hour drive to Feodosia, Cory stopped the car in a rural spot and pointed to some bushes.

Anya helped us take the interns to a dolphin show their first weekend with us. On our thirty-minute drive, we passed gorgeous scenery: hills, valleys, vineyards, farmland, and jagged volcanic ridges. Anya pointed out the village where she had lived as a child and later taught school.

The vineyards, she explained, were destroyed about eighty years ago in a campaign against alcoholism. Without grapes, people simply found other sources of alcohol—some of them quite deadly. Most of the vineyards had since been replanted and winemaking became a major industry.

Anya said the dolphin station was once a top-secret military project with no visitors allowed. They trained dolphins to swim to enemy ships wearing explosives. After the Cold War, the center became a tourist attraction.

Still, it's no Sea World. No signs marked the way. We found no gift shop or snack bar, though a few old women sold cabbage-filled pastries by the gate. The buildings showed years of neglect but the setting was beautiful. It lay close to the beach, surrounded by trees and jagged volcanic crags.

For the show, we crowded around a swimming pool in the dolphin building. First, two seals played with balls and retrieved rings tossed into the water. Then a dolphin performed. Seeing the dolphin leap gracefully, something so beautiful in a country so severe, made me feel like crying.

Tatiana gave the interns a crash course in Russian, and they started meeting with English speaking students at School Number Two. Over twenty teens came three times a week to play games and discuss different topics. They talked about hobbies and holidays, life in America, and Ukrainian culture. The head English teacher told me her students really liked it, and she was pleased with their improved English skills.

Tatiana also arranged for the interns to come to the Lingua Club, a place she worked part-time teaching English. The children's teacher there, a vibrant Christian, encouraged them to talk about their faith. Tatiana also asked them to share their testimonies in her adult class.

Since the interns could not "proselytize" at school, they invited students to a Bible study held at a different time at Anya's apartment. Three came from the school and one girl came from Lingua Club.

Early in July, a team of four flew from Wichita, Kansas to help lead a day camp. They came well prepared with crafts, sports equipment, games, Bible stories, and a clown outfit. Workers from the Feodosia church, mostly teen-age girls, helped lead Bible lessons and songs. Several women prepared snacks and a lunch each day for fifty-five children.

The following week, Cory and the interns provided the "exotic" American entertainment for a second group of sixty kids. On Friday afternoon, campers put on a closing program for their parents. The campers and workers sang and gave skits for almost two hours. Many songs were the same ones I once sang at camp, only in Russian. "I've got the joy, joy, joy, joy down in my heart." Their enthusiasm provided great contrast to the pessimism I heard daily around town.

For two years, I bought light bulbs from a woman named Inga at the hardware store. Though she gave her usual scowl to most customers, she smiled when she saw me coming, and I chatted with her if she wasn't busy. She complained that her children didn't have anything to do that summer, so I told her about the camp. She decided to send her seven-year-old son Vlad.

I met Inga and little Vlad in order to walk them to the camp held at the old church property on the hill, the place we lived when we first came to Feodosia. Vlad wore a scowl and dragged his feet the whole way. Upon arrival, Vlad cried with his face in Mama's skirt. Inga looked nervous too, then relieved when she saw her former schoolteacher.

I stayed until 11:00, helped in the kitchen and checked on Vlad. On my way home, I let Inga know her son was doing fine.

"Thank you," she said with a look of relief.

The next morning, she brought me a three-liter jar of milk still warm from their cow. Vlad was quite a different little boy and told me with a twinkle in his eye, "I didn't know Pioneer camp would be so much fun!"

Inga thanked me again for letting her son come to camp. "He hated day care since the workers yelled at the children. He doesn't like school either, but he likes this camp very much. He got ready early this morning and kept saying, 'Come on, Mama, it's time to go.'"

Inga asked me many questions about our church and what we believe. "Where do you meet?" I gave her the address. She asked about her former teacher. "Alla goes there too? She used to tell us there is no God."

I later asked Alla how she became a Christian.

"I used to live next door to the church when it was up on the hill," she said. "I could hear them sing. Sometimes I'd stand outside and listen through the window."

Stefan's family lived on that property then, and Alla taught Stefan's girls in school. "They were such good girls," she recalled. "I watched their family. My husband was a drunk, but Stefan came home every evening at 5:00 to work around the house."

Someone invited Alla to an evangelistic festival three years earlier when a group came from Kansas. She attended and went forward to repent. Until this year, however, she rarely attended church services. "But now," she said, "I want to live for God." She planned to be baptized later that month in a service at the Black Sea.

Tatiana called from the maternity hospital. In a desperate voice, she asked, "Will you pray for me?" She had irregular contractions a few days and was concerned things weren't progressing fast enough.

I packed a snack and water, since the hospital couldn't afford to feed the patients, and went to visit her. A nurse stopped me at the door of the three-story building and then brought Tatiana out to see me.

"I'm glad you came," she said. "I just wanted to hear your voice." We walked around the courtyard for an hour or so, stopping occasionally so she could concentrate on breathing. She said the breathing exercise I taught her helped a lot.

This wasn't the first time she had been admitted to the maternity hospital. The doctor told her to check in a whole week before her due date. Since her husband, Victor, had to bring all her food, she preferred to stay home. After a couple days, they let her go home again, because of a dysentery outbreak at the hospital.

Tatiana told me, "When Victor comes to visit, he throws rocks at my window, like a school-boy. The other women in my room are surprised to see a man standing there with gray hair. I don't tell them how old I am."

When I visited her the next day, she couldn't come out to play, but they did let her talk to me out the window of her third-floor room—still no baby but some progress. Victor called that evening to say she had given birth to a girl around 5:00 pm. He sounded excited.

Tatiana had told me earlier, "After Victor spent time with Janelle and Alicia, he decided a girl might not be bad. He already has two boys anyway." His sons, from a previous marriage, lived with their mother. "When we were looking for a used baby stroller, someone tried to sell us a very old one with holes in it. Victor told them, 'What? And have the boy babies looking in at my little girl?'"

Cory, the girls and I visited Tatiana the next day, but we couldn't go up to see her. She poked her head out of her third-floor window and explained that even Victor wouldn't see his daughter until they went home. That would be a week, at least.

I brought fried chicken for her. She dropped a bag attached to a rope so I could send it up. One is supposed to give food to the food attendant, but Victor had a creative streak and besides, he couldn't always come before she went home at 5:00.

The outside walls of the maternity home were marked with graffiti at ground level. Proud fathers and relatives had scratched birth announcements in the plaster, such as: "I have a son" followed by the date, or simply a name and a date.

Two weeks later, I visited Tatiana and baby Olla at home. They lived in something like a dorm, sharing a kitchen and bathroom with numerous other families. When I entered their room, I felt as if I'd walked into a well-packed storage closet. The first half of the room contained a small refrigerator, a table, and shelves for dishes and food. The other half had a crib, a bed, a desk, and shelves to the ceiling packed with Tatiana's many books. Very little floor showed.

She had told me earlier about her housing woes. Many years before their marriage, she had signed up with the "Department of Housing" to get an apartment. In the USSR, everyone was supposed to receive free housing, free medical care, and free schooling. She never did get her apartment.

She once lived with her mother and stepfather, helping them fix up and furnish their house with her wages. After her mother died and Tatiana got married, her stepfather told her to move out. She and Victor couldn't afford to rent an apartment like ours. Our rent, $110, was more than their combined salary.

I had asked her, "Do you still have any hope of getting an apartment through the Department of Housing? I know the government isn't building new apartment buildings, but old people die and many emigrate."

"No," she had said, "most apartments are privatized now, and the mafia is able to get any apartments which do become available." So they coped with what they had.

Tatiana pulled out a chair for me and plunked her teakettle on a table-top burner. "Will you have some tea with us?"

Her baby slept, but she gently lifted a blanket covering the crib so I could peek. "Olla may look like me," said Victor with a proud grin, "but she has her mother's temperament...especially when she cries!"

Over tea, Tatiana gave me the full story, the one she didn't want to shout out the window from the third floor. She was glad she had hired a nurse to be with her at the hospital. The doctor on duty did not want the responsibility of overseeing Tatiana's delivery, since she was "too old." He wanted to get a surgeon to perform a cesarean.

The nurse kept Tatiana in the labor room and had her start pushing in secret—so when she went to the delivery room, (they told her to run there) it was already too late for a caesarean. It sounded all very traumatic, but she delivered without any complications. She felt so relieved when she heard her baby cry for the first time.

There was only one toilet on her floor and often they had no running water. "We are patient women," she said. "We know how to wait."

I enjoyed breaks from housework, but I couldn't be away much. Clothes didn't wash themselves, and I needed to can in preparation for winter. Having grown up in the country, the big outdoors was my backyard, and I felt sorry that Janelle and Alicia couldn't play outside any time they wanted. My neighbors warned me against leaving them alone outside. "Times have changed," one said. Anya told me some kidnapping stories.

Though I didn't have much time to sit outside with them, I decided they weren't too deprived. While I stood over the sink, stove, or washing machine, they found things to do inside. They built dollhouses with Legos or played Noah's ark with their stuffed animals. They colored and played educational computer games. They put chair cushions on the floor and jumped on them from the couch. Cushions on the floor made it quieter for "doing exercises" since we tried to be considerate of the folks downstairs. Sometimes I made them a tent, draping a sheet over chairs.

They liked to mop the floor until they had done it a few times and it became too much like work. They helped me can pickles by washing cucumbers and stuffing dill in the jars. When we had a heat wave, our bathtub became a wading pool. They gave their dolls—and the floor—a bath. We ate a picnic lunch on the balcony.

My sister wrote to say that her girls missed playing with my girls when they visited Grandma's house. I read the letter to Janelle and Alicia.

"Will we see them again when we go to Grandma's house?" Alicia asked. "But then we will be too big to play. We will be mamas then." When you are not quite four, two more years seems like forever.

Five-year-old Janelle said, "You have to be really old when you get married. I'm going to get married when I am ten."

Janelle and Alicia discussed the size of Stefan's family one day. "They have five children," noted Janelle. "I wonder how Stefan and Nadia take care of them?"

Alicia suggested, "Maybe they brush their teeth by themselves."

At one time, I wondered if my babies would ever become potty trained. They grew older and I wondered if they would ever learn to tie their shoes. Then it clicked and they spent the rest of the day looking for shoes and strings they could use for practice.

Cory came home that evening and reported on the brothers' meeting. "Igor says they should be more careful who they baptize this year, since most of the people baptized last year no longer attend."

Cory thought the problem wasn't with the new converts but with poor "parenting." He later preached on the topic of discipleship. He compared new Christians to babies. Parents don't expect babies to cook, wash clothes, and figure out everything alone. Parents spend a lot of time caring for the new member of the family. He stressed that all believers are to "go and make disciples"—it's not just the job of the pastor or church leaders.

- 19 -
"Don't Worry, It Will Get Worse"

I grew up hearing stories about the persecuted church behind the Iron Curtain. I thought Russian Christians must be as close to sainthood as you can get. I often heard, "The best thing that could happen to American churches is the purifying fire of persecution." I moved behind the former Iron Curtain and learned Russian believers aren't perfect either.

I came across an article in the May 1997 issue of *Christianity Today* called, "Is Persecution Good for the Church?" The author, Mark Gallit, wrote that the blood of martyrs can strengthen the church, but it doesn't always. Persecution can crush the church. Never-ending repression stifles evangelism and the church declines. He said that those who speak of the "purity" of the persecuted church probably haven't seen it up close.

From our experience, we agree. Believers in the Soviet Union had lived with self-preservation as their focus for so long, the church had a hard time breaking out of that mindset. In the absence of Bibles, preachers taught traditions. Spirituality was often judged by conformity to external things such as head coverings, simple dress, and a certain hairstyle. Church members viewed outsiders with suspicion.

The church council decided to remove Anya from her position as Sunday School director because she wore makeup. A couple weeks later, they held a members' meeting and announced the decision.

Anya joined the girls and me for a walk to the Black Sea. While the girls played in the waves, Anya poured out her troubles. "I've worked so hard for that church," she said. "I've given so much. Maybe it's better if I sit back and don't do anything." Her chin quivered and her voice cracked.

"I know it's not a sin to wear makeup. The Bible doesn't say that." She felt that some simply didn't like her.

She said she visited the charismatic church and people greeted her so warmly. "But I can't leave my church," she cried. "This is where I was baptized. It's my home church."

I'd heard criticism of the charismatic church for "sheep stealing." Some sheep, I observed, were pushed from the fold.

Anya sank into deeper depression as the week went on. Cory encouraged her to persevere. "You are gifted with children," he told her. "And you know how to make people feel welcome. You know what it's like to be in the world. Maybe you can start a Good News Club for children or a Bible study for non-Christians."

The next Sunday, Anya walked to church wearing a smile, a fake-pearl necklace, a bright pink hat, and matching lipstick. The much quoted verse, 1 Peter 3:3, doesn't say women can't wear fake pearls or lipstick, just no gold. And she did have a head covering.

I discussed the makeup controversy with two women in the church. Older believers had trained them on proper attire and conduct soon after they became Christians. They thought headscarves were ugly but wore them anyway to avoid offending others.

I said, "Those who don't wear makeup and those who do just need to love one another. After all, Jesus said people will know we are Christians 'by our love,' not by what we look like."

It's not that simple, I learned. One woman explained that conservative members quoted other scriptures, saying, "It's better to have a mill stone hung around your neck and be drowned in the sea than to cause one of these little ones to stumble."

I had to wonder though, are the longtime believers so fragile in their faith they are tempted to run out and don makeup? The makeup-wearing newcomers left the church, not the charter members.

Cory, Andre, and Stefan continued to meet to discuss how they might train people to plant churches. Andre felt they needed many new churches around Crimea. Cory reminded him the existing churches would feel threatened by new churches.

"Some people will criticize no matter what you do," Andre said. Nevertheless, he laid the foundation carefully.

In July, Andre held his third seminar for leaders from regional churches. He knew not everyone would want to plant new churches, but he wanted to impart vision and minimize resistance. The seminars also gave Andre the opportunity to see who was motivated for church planting and evangelism.

In that seminar, Andre focused on basic doctrine. How does someone know he is saved? How do you talk to a nonbeliever about faith in God? If someone wants to be forgiven, how do you counsel him? Do you just tell him to go to church, sit through a service, and go forward at the end?

"Next seminar," Andre said, "we will talk more about methods of reaching nonbelievers, like small-group Bible studies. We have thirty men here today. If each of you started a Bible study for non-Christians, that could potentially make thirty new churches." This was his first hint to the group that he would like to see believers plant many new churches.

Though the meeting was held in Feodosia, only three men from the Feodosia church attended: Cory, Stefan, and Vladimir Alexandrovich. We had come to Ukraine to work with the Feodosia church, but we could see the value of working regionally.

One young pastor attending the seminars asked Cory to provide "limousine service" for his wedding. When Cory reached Ivan's village home, the groom wasn't ready, and they arrived late to everything all day.

They stopped first at the bride's house. Was she standing at the door ready to go? No. Ivan and his party followed the custom of looking through the house until they found her. Though already time for the civil ceremony, they all sat down to eat breakfast.

The official wedding in Ukraine must take place in a government office, not a church. They signed papers in a dingy gray building next to a cow pasture. The woman in charge rattled off her canned speech while the bust of Lenin looked on.

Next they stopped to greet Ivan's congregation before driving to the girl's village. The two-hour service at her church included special music and a long evangelistic sermon aimed at the nonbelievers in the audience.

At 3:00, around one hundred guests sat down at long tables to eat the wedding feast. The meal and entertainment lasted five hours. After dinner, friends presented the couple with songs, funny skits, poems, gifts, and words of congratulations.

"I wish you health and happiness," many said. "And don't forget your parents."

One skit imitated them after twenty-five years. Old Ivan took a handkerchief out of his pocket and blew his nose, folded it up, and put it in his pocket again. Old Yula asked, "Do you always fold your hankie?"

"Yes," he replied.

"All these years, I thought you never used your hankies, so I just put them back on the shelf."

"So that's why they are always stiff."

"Just goes to show that we're still learning about each other after all these years."

Cory joined a short-term team from North Carolina for their evangelistic outreach in the village of Simisotki (translated Seven-hundred). It had a population of something like three or four thousand people but no church and no known believers.

About 150 people came to the meeting held in the Cultural Hall. Cory noted a poem painted in large letters on the wall. The poem extolled the virtues of kind Father Lenin: "He is always with us." When Cory preached, he referred to it. "Lenin is not always with us, but God is." He explained the message of John 3:16. Two other men also preached. Almost every adult came forward at the invitation.

"These people have never, ever heard the gospel before," he told me later. "They haven't even had the opportunity. Maybe we've made a mistake by focusing on the cities and neglecting the villages."

Cory and Stefan planned to follow-up in Simisotki with a showing of the *Jesus* film in early August. In preparation for the event, they hung one hundred posters around town. Most were ripped down, but around seventy people still attended the film, about fifty adults and twenty kids.

After the film, the children jumped over chairs and *ran* out to the car where Stefan passed out Bibles. Adults followed behind. Stefan and Cory gave away sixty New Testaments.

Cory met with Andre and Stefan often and liked the camaraderie he felt with these men. Since neither had a telephone, if their meeting wasn't scheduled in advance, they simply dropped in on each other.

Stefan lived in town, but Andre lived in a small village near Feodosia. He was butchering a cow when Cory went to see him one day. While Andre cut up the stomach to feed to his dogs, they discussed leadership training and animal sounds. Russian dogs say, "Guf, guf." American dogs say, "Woof, woof." Which one is right? They never did decide.

During one visit, the neighbor's dogs howled non-stop. "My neighbor is a spiritist," Andre explained. "Her dogs always act like that when she holds a séance." His own dogs stayed calm.

Cory learned more about Andre and how he became a Christian. His grandfather had been a believer and was respected by many his village. Andre grew up in Russia in a non-Christian home.

He went to university in Moscow and lived as other nonbelievers, drinking and carousing. There he met his wife, Delara, a Volga Tatar of nominal Muslim background. They graduated as geologists and went to work in Uzbekistan for two years.

They later moved to Feodosia together. Andre went to visit his grandfather, back in Russia, seeking a loan for a house and land. He wanted to start a business growing tomatoes for sale. Grandpa gave him money and a Bible. Andre read the Bible and wrote a letter to Grandpa, asking many questions. The old man sent him the address of a church in Feodosia. Andre attended and after several months, he gave his life to Christ.

Since Sunday was the biggest market day of the week, Andre's ripe tomatoes conflicted with church attendance. "I felt that God wanted me to stop selling tomatoes on Sunday," he said, "but I didn't know how I would make a living. I obeyed and God blessed me. I sold more on Monday, even though it's usually a slow market day. People stood in line for my tomatoes."

He had been a Christian only a couple years when the small church in Sudak needed a pastor. Someone suggested Andre, and the other brothers agreed; no one else wanted to go. Sudak was over an hour from his home. When he had a working car, he drove, otherwise, he hitchhiked.

"I felt so inadequate," Andre said. "I didn't know what I was doing and I didn't feel I was gifted to be a pastor." A teenager named Romon started attending the Sudak church. Andre saw he had an open heart. They spent much time together and Romon gave his life to Christ.

Andre wanted more training and started going to Moscow for seminars. Meanwhile, he mentored Romon, who grew quickly as a Christian.

Andre had led the Sudak congregation for four or five years when he felt Romon, age twenty-three, had matured enough to take over as pastor. Andre passed the mantle and received a new assignment. The Crimean council elected him as overseer for the churches of Eastern Crimea.

Andre, Stefan, and Cory decided the best way to plant new churches was to start evangelistic Bible studies meeting in homes. When the group grew to fifteen to twenty people, it should divide into two groups. The leader would disciple new believers to help them learn to lead.

They agreed the house-church model would be more effective than trying to build a bunch of church buildings. Andre said, "If we go through another time of persecution authorities can easily confiscate a big church building. It's harder to stop house churches."

They outlined a training program for church planters and planned to start in five months, after the holidays in January. Andre had noticed twenty young men he thought might make good church planters, but decided they should start with only ten.

They didn't want to duplicate the traditional Bible college method and remove the men from their home villages for long periods. They decided it would be better to have participants attend lectures for four days every other week, then return home to put the teaching into practice. They would provide a stipend for two years while the church planters focused on learning and starting cell-groups.

They wanted to make the training as practical as possible. Lectures would include some theory, but the goal was to plant churches, not simply train men in church planting. They decided to give homework assignments designed to help the students start small groups.

Leaders of the program would visit the church planters to provide on-site mentoring. They decided to invite three other progressive pastors to help teach and mentor—one of them was Romon from Sudak, the young man Andre had discipled.

We were so grateful God brought us together with visionary men who wanted to start new churches. Cory hoped for a church planting movement but knew he couldn't do it on his own. He also thought it would be better if it were Russian-led, with him taking a support role. Locals knew the culture better, but he could provide some outside perspective.

Andre was widely respected by church leaders in the region, at least most respected him. When he told the Feodosia church council about their plans for training church planters, he got a hostile response. Igor accused him of meeting in secret and told him, "You need to get advice from those with more experience."

Andre said, "I'm listening."

Igor criticized Andre, Stefan, and Cory at length. He said Andre and Stefan were chasing American money. They were traitors. Stefan was lazy. Andre wanted to take over as pastor. Cory was a traitor too. He was supposed to help the Feodosia church but worked against it instead. He didn't understand the culture or respect Ukrainian church traditions.

After that meeting, Andre told Cory, "We have a Russian saying, 'Don't worry, it will get worse.'"

- 20 -
Thankful for Candles

School in Ukraine started every year on September 1, no matter what day of the week it fell. Flower vendors did good business on that day, since students took flowers to their teachers for the first day of school. After school began, classes were held Monday through Friday.

I resumed home school lessons for Janelle, officially in kindergarten, and Alicia, in preschool. Actually, we "did school" off and on all summer since they enjoyed the extra attention and structured activity.

I made them a number chart, in rows of ten up to one hundred. They could count to twenty, even twenty-nine—but what comes after twenty-nine...twenty-ten?

Their favorite part of school was getting to glue something to a letter of the alphabet. We did apple peelings for "A." Beans for "B." They collected leaves to glue on the letter "L."

Cooler weather brought out brilliant hues on the trees in our courtyard. The ivy on our building turned red. Seeing seasons change through the eyes of a child brought a fresh sense of wonder and excitement.

"Look at this leaf! Look at this one!! And this one!!" They took their colorful treasures inside and made leaf pictures and leaf bouquets.

In a few short weeks, we went from t-shirts to sweatshirts during the day and from sheet-only to two blankets at night. We had entered the long hurry-up-and-get-dressed-before-you-get-cold season.

I didn't have time to teach school every day with canning season still in progress. Though other housewives canned great quantities of cooked green pepper relish, I preferred to get my vitamins from grape juice. Crimea had many vineyards but didn't produce grape juice, only wine. Imported juice cost something like $1.10 for a one-liter box at the market.

Growing up on the farm, I learned to be a hard-core penny-pincher. I went to the market and lugged home forty pounds of grapes. Janelle and Alicia helped pluck the fruit off the stems and washed them in big washtubs. As I crimped the lid of my thirteenth liter of concentrate, I calculated my savings, about $70. Not bad for a morning's work.

There was a drawback, however. When I was canning along in high gear, the rest of the house got untidy; or maybe I should say it was worse than usual.

A woman from the Primorski church kindly stopped in with a three-liter jar of fresh milk from her cow. I took a break from wiping grape-juice spatters off the wall and shoved things over on the couch so she could sit down.

"Your apartment is so…clean," she said. I would not have chosen that adjective.

Though strangers didn't look us in the eye or smile, we were surrounded by nice people. When I bought more grapes one day, the woman selling them asked, "Where are you from?"

"America," I said. That always shocked them.

She gave me extra saying, "I don't want you to think Russians are stingy."

I lugged my load home and exchanged nods with the neighborhood "watchdog," the old woman on the first floor. The teenage boy who lived upstairs came from behind me, silently grabbed my heavy bags, and hauled them up to the fourth floor.

"Thank you," I said, when he set them down at my door.

"It's nothing," he replied. I decided I could put up with his loud rock music.

Those who move to or travel in a different country often fear others will take advantage of them. I did at first, but I found many kind folk. People have picked up and returned money I unknowingly dropped.

I found a cheese vendor at the market with good cheese. One day, I paid her with a 20-hryvna bill (about $12) but forgot to wait for change and spent the rest of the day wondering what happened to my money. When I bought cheese several weeks later, the lady told me she owed me money. The change was equivalent to one-week's wage for some.

I took her homemade chocolate chip cookies later. She asked for the recipe. Relationships took time to build, but they were build-able.

I could talk about most things in Russian, but sometimes I liked jabbering in English with Tatiana. I took the girls to visit her and baby Olla occasionally. We rode the bus to her hostel and walked down the dark corridor to her room. Light bulbs installed in the hall always disappeared.

"Be careful," she said when she opened the door one day. I didn't know what I was supposed to be careful of, and stepped in some doggie droppings. She explained that other residents in the building didn't put their dogs outside, so she had a "present" at her door every morning.

I showed her how to use the diapers I gave her. The doctor had taught her to wrap a cloth tightly around the baby from the shoulders down.

"That way is old fashioned," Tatiana told me. "I've been wrapping her from the waist down." Both methods, though, resulted in wet bedding. Since the water was frequently off, she couldn't wash often.

She showed me a photo. "I found this old picture of my mother holding me when I was a baby," she said.

"Your mother looks so young!" I commented.

"She wasn't really that young, just very thin. You see, even ten years after the war, (World War II) food was still scarce and most people were hungry all the time."

After her mother graduated from college, she decided to accept a position in Feodosia because she heard tomatoes were plentiful and cheap there during the summer. Fresh fruit and vegetables were rare in Moscow. Even though bread was scarce in Feodosia, she liked the idea of being able to eat all the tomatoes she wanted. She moved to Feodosia and got sores in her mouth from eating too many.

Conversations I overheard around town focused on economic hardships. "I used to work at the ship factory and got a good salary, but it's closed now. Most factories are closed. Where is anyone supposed to find work?"

"I receive 49 hryvna (about $20) a month for my pension. What's 49 hryvna? That will buy one loaf of bread a day and a bottle of cooking gas. Nothing more. How are we supposed to live?"

"I can't afford meat or butter or fat. We don't have heat or hot water. I watch the news on TV and wonder how much worse can it get...and how will it ever get better?"

I could hear anger, frustration, and fear in their voices. Casual conversations with neighbors often turned to the subject of economic hardship. One person said, "The only freedom we have is the freedom to starve."

I heard of a local woman, a teacher, who did starve to death. She had not received any salary for a long time and was too proud to ask anyone for help.

On my way to the market one day, I met our sweet neighbor lady coming home with two bags of apples. Potatoes were expensive because of the heavy rains that summer.

"Apples are abundant and cheap this year," she said cheerfully. "We'll just eat more apples."

She once worked as a seamstress, but the clothing factory had closed. She received no pay for the work she did during her final year there.

"I read that Kiev promised to get back-wages and pensions caught up by the end of the year," I said. "Have you heard that too?"

"City council members just line their pockets," she replied, shaking her head. "None of us will see the money."

Most people ate meat only once a week, if that much. I wondered, *Are we extravagant to eat it every day?*

Before coming to Ukraine we read a book that encouraged missionaries to bond with the locals by living as they do. It seemed like good advice —we didn't want to live much higher than those around us. Because of the abject poverty, I felt uncomfortable spending much money.

I think we were right to start out as simple as possible, but economizing in some areas just made it harder on us and didn't help anyone else. I decided it's okay to eat meat every day and heat my bath water every night. We didn't live extravagantly, but we could eat good food and stay warm and I didn't have to feel guilty about it.

We saw some very large, very nice houses going up around town and heard that they belonged to businessmen, mafia members, and members of the city council. Feodosia had rich people too, but most people looked down on them.

Though many associated profit and wealth with dishonesty, a new middle-class appeared. Communism had fostered reliance on the State, but younger people found innovative ways to make money.

Cory met a businessman who said he earned some $2000 during the summer as a middleman changing money, then he worked as a mechanic the rest of the year. He told Cory, "I was eighteen years old when Gorbachev was president and the USSR started to break apart. I don't think like my parents do."

Still, we lived with the results of a bankrupt system. After the electricity went off one evening, Janelle and Alicia wanted a snack. By the light of a candle, I buttered a piece of bread and sprinkled cinnamon and sugar on it—or at least I thought I did. I kept the cinnamon-sugar mixture in a plastic spice container and salt in a similar shaker.

Janelle was not impressed with the generous layer of salt on her bread. "I would NEVER do that to MY children," she said indignantly. "I'm going to tell my kids what you did."

Washing clothes was always a time-intensive task, but one day was more frustrating than usual. The wash side of the machine leaked water into the centrifuge side so the centrifuge would not work. I scooped water out. The basin slipped and sloshed water all over the floor. I mopped up the mess, washed, scooped, rinsed, and hung clothes outside the balcony. I found a hole in a new t-shirt. *Grrr.* That washing machine thrashed our clothes. Then the electricity went out. I wasn't done yet!

The girls had been watching the movie, *Pollyanna*, about the girl who always looked for the bright side. I thought about her and tried to discipline my mind. *I'm glad we have a washing machine since it's easier than washing by hand. I'm glad I got some clothes washed before the electricity failed.* The Bible said it another way, "In everything give thanks."

When I was younger, I thought it would have been fun to live in the time of Laura Ingalls Wilder. My fantasy died in Ukraine. My grandparents had lives more difficult than mine, but they weren't bitter people.

Though my Grandma Brown felt constant pain before she died at age ninety-six, she expressed gratitude and joy every time I visited her. She rarely got out and couldn't see well but often chirped, "It's so beautiful outside today!"

It started to rain on the laundry I'd hung out. Growl. *I'm glad we have a heater so I can dry clothes inside.* I tried to follow Grandma's example and look for the good.

At bedtime, Alicia said, "I wish I was a bird."

"Why do you want to be a bird?" I asked.

"So I could lay eggs...and I could fly. I would fly to Grandma and Grandpa's house."

Janelle said, "If I could have anything, I'd want a big house, like Uncle Mike and Aunt Linda's. I wouldn't have to be quiet then."

I didn't tell them, but I wanted to fly away too. I also wanted a big house with pretty things, hot water, and an automatic washing machine.

Cory doesn't like to travel, but his work kept him on the road. I'm more adventurous, but my job kept me at home. I jumped at the chance for a trip when a friend from Oregon invited me to visit her in Kiev early in November. Stefan had to go to Kiev anyway, so he accompanied me on the train.

My friend Vicky Hoffman and her interpreter met me at the Kiev train station and took me sightseeing. Our tour included a park near the Dneiper River featuring the statue of Vladimir.

A little over one thousand years ago, the ruler of Kiev, Vladimir, decided his heathen citizens needed a civilized religion. He sent a delegation to investigate the major religions of the world.

They returned later and said the Jews had many rules and couldn't eat pork. The Muslims couldn't eat pork either and had to take off their shoes to pray. The Orthodox Christians, though, had an awe-inspiring cathedral in Constantinople and beautiful rituals.

Vladimir chose Christianity to be the state religion and baptized his people in the Dneiper River. Those refusing baptism were killed unless they could escape. The Russian Orthodox consider Vladimir a saint.

We visited a 900-year-old monastery complex, which included underground catacombs that provide the final resting place for many mummified monks. These monks achieved sainthood status through acts of self-denial, such as fasting and living in caves.

Some say you can tell they were real saints because their bodies didn't decay like normal, but dried instead. Skeptics, however, say the special type of dirt in the cave simply sucked the moisture from their bodies while the cool cave temperature preserved them. Nevertheless, some believe that those who touch one of these mummified saints will receive immediate healing; Orthodox believers made pilgrimages there to pray.

We stopped outside the cave building to read the long list of rules. This is a holy place. No sleeveless shirts, no shorts, no hats on men. No talking, only praying. Consider your life and where you will go after death.

We bought candles and descended into the underground labyrinth. Coffins rested on benches built into the cave walls. Through the glass cover of each coffin, I could see a body-shape covered with fancy cloth from head to toe. Since the saints were well protected, no one could actually touch them to try to get healing, but I saw one woman kiss a coffin.

I stayed up late that night talking to Vicky. "It has been a lot harder for us to live in Ukraine than we expected," I told her from my mattress on the floor of her room. "Our mission organization wants to know if we plan to come back for another term, but we don't know what to tell them."

I described our living conditions in Feodosia, then said, "For a while, I thought, 'I'll complete this term, so we can save face with our supporters, but I'll never come back to Feodosia again. I don't even care or want to know what God thinks about it.' That sounded unspiritual, so I changed it to: 'I'll come back if God gives me the desire to come back.' That sounds safe enough."

Vicky laughed.

"I am able to live here," I continued. "I know how to go shopping and I know Russian now, but I don't like living here. It's hard. I have done difficult things before, like when I was in Kenya, but I always wanted to do them."

Vicky had known me for many years and understood. "Is there something else you feel God is calling you to do?" she asked.

"No, I just want a nicer house and an easier lifestyle. It's hard being so far from my family, especially since I have children now and they grow up so fast and they don't get to see their grandparents and cousins."

"Does Cory like it here?"

"No. It's hard for him, too."

Vicky admitted she didn't have many answers for me. "I know God is a shepherd who takes care of His sheep. But I also know God sometimes asks us to do difficult things. I don't think you can make a decision based on whether or not something is hard. God knows how much you can handle, and He can make up for the difference."

The trip to Kiev gave me food for thought in the following weeks. I had seen caves where monks hid from the world and suffered just for the sake of suffering, it seemed. Why couldn't I accept hardship with joy when my journey to the world included suffering for the sake of Christ? I knew what it said in First Peter, chapter one, about rejoicing in trials.

A younger Peter also tried to avoid the path of suffering. When Jesus said he must go to Jerusalem to die, Peter tried to redirect the Savior. At Jesus' trial, Peter denied knowing Jesus, fearing for his own life.

Jesus told Peter, "You are used to doing what you want now, but when you are old, someone else will take you where you do not want to go" (my paraphrase of John 21:18). Sure enough, Peter's independent spirit was tamed, and he learned to accept suffering as a part of his walk with Christ. In all five chapters of First Peter, he wrote about suffering as though it's a normal part of Christianity.

Power and water outages helped us appreciate simple pleasures, like electricity and water. More than once I peeled potatoes by kerosene lamplight and boiled them on our gas stove. We ate dinner with a candle flickering on our table.

"I'm thankful for candles," I said one evening.

Janelle joined in with a hearty, "Amen!"

Alicia said, "I'm thankful for my mommy and daddy."

"Amen!" they said together.

"I'm thankful for my girls."

"AMEN!" we all shouted.

"I'm thankful for our heater."

Without electricity, I lost the urge to jump up and wash dishes or be productive. We continued to count our blessings. We gave thanks for spoons, potatoes, beds, doors, chairs, keys, clothes, toys—and shouted "AMEN!" between each one.

It was a good start to rejoicing in trial, but I still wasn't ready to sign up for another term. I *was* ready to hear God's perspective, though. I later jotted in my journal:

"...they first gave themselves to the Lord and to us by the will of God" (2 Cor. 8:5). It's of no value to simply give ourselves to the work of the Lord. We must give ourselves to the Lord first, and then to whatever, wherever He directs.

Lord, I don't know how else to give myself to You. I don't want to run from this place out of personal dislike or stay out of a misguided sense of duty. I can only put myself in Your hands. I want my roots to go deep into Your water of life so I might not wither in this dry land.

Do you have anything to say, Lord?

I wanted a sense of whether or not we should return to Ukraine. The only thought which came to mind, however, was: *I love you...and My plans for you are for a future and a hope.* I realized God was more interested in my relationship with Him, than what I did for Him. I continued to write:

I've been like a child who drags her feet and screams, "I don't want to go!" That alone takes so much energy. I'd rather walk willingly and peacefully by Your side, holding Your hand, and trusting You will carry me in the places that are too difficult for me. I acknowledge that You are big enough to carry me and You love me enough to do that.

- 21 -
Heart Trouble

Late in November, Andre held his fifth meeting for leaders of area churches, still wanting to broaden their vision for reaching beyond church walls. This meeting became sidetracked, however. The elderly head of the Baptist Union for Crimea came from Simferopol, took the floor and talked on and on.

He emphasized the need to preserve the "true faith" and church traditions. When he spoke against makeup, one new Christian asked, "Where does it say in the Bible that makeup is a sin?" The old man answered by stressing the need to respect church customs.

Andre never did cover what he hoped to and closed the meeting saying, "We will look at our traditions in the next meeting, in January. We will look at which are simply traditions and which are Biblical."

Cory came home, told me about the meeting and said, "I have that tightness in my chest again. My heartbeat is irregular, too. Here, feel my pulse."

Sure enough, his pulse felt irregular to me, too.

Cory called an American nurse in Simferopol who ran a clinic in her home with the help of a Russian doctor. "I've had these symptoms for several weeks now," he told her.

"Come on over," she said. "We'll check you out."

The next day, the doctor gave Cory a thorough exam and a cardiogram. He concluded Cory had a stress-induced arrhythmia, or irregular heartbeat. The doctor encouraged him to walk a lot and drink warm milk before going to bed. We consulted an American doctor over e-mail and got a similar diagnosis.

Cory had been under a lot of stress. He found church politics even more difficult than cultural adjustments and language learning. Tensions continued with Igor. Cory tried to work things out with him but received a hostile response. The church planters' training program seemed like a good idea, but that too faced opposition and so many things could go wrong.

Cory started walking along the waterfront every morning and used the time for prayer and praise. It helped. He also decided to cut back on activities at the Feodosia church and focus his energy on developing the training program.

He continued to meet often with Andre and Stefan. Each member of this leadership team brought different ideas, yet a sense of unity and goodwill reigned. That fall, they had begun to meet weekly with three more men who would help share the teaching load. They discussed which topics they should cover and planned who would give each lecture.

Cory showed me their list of topics, which included God's desire to reach the world, basic doctrine, personal character development, what is the church, evangelism, and discipleship.

In our home school, Janelle and Alicia made sheep with cardboard and cotton balls and learned the first part of Psalm 23. Alicia came up with a new version: "The Lord is my shepherd, I shall not want. The sheep's in the meadow, the cow's in the corn."

I had my own craft project. Janelle and Alicia needed wide hair bands that could pull their hair back while their bangs grew out. I decided the elastic I had cut off an old pair of Cory's underwear would work nicely, and covered it with pretty material.

Needing elastic for a second hair band, I searched for more rag material. "Cory has too much underwear anyway," I decided. "He won't miss this one."

I'm not sure Cory shared my enthusiasm. "I want you to know that's my favorite brand," he said as I snipped off the precious hair-band elastic.

The next day I found some wide elastic at the market, so Cory didn't have to hide the rest of his underwear.

On Christmas Eve, the girls unwrapped gift teddy bears they named Holly and Christmas Bear. They tossed their favorite dolls out of bed and the newcomers got the honored place in their arms for the night.

When Janelle emerged from her bedroom the next morning holding her bear, she said, "I told Holly all about how Jesus was born and that Christmas is His birthday."

On the last Sunday of December, Anya walked to church with us. She had missed quite a few Sundays and cried during most of our twenty-minute walk to church. "It's like when a child gets hurt visiting the doctor," she said. "After that, he starts screaming whenever he sees a white coat. I feel that way about church. I had no peace in the world and thought I would find it in church. But there is no peace, no love. It's cold."

That summer, she had been dismissed as a Sunday School teacher for wearing makeup. In the fall, Igor summoned her to a brothers' meeting and reviewed her faults. Because she continued to wear makeup, she was now guilty of rebellion. She felt that Igor simply didn't like her.

What could I say? I had already urged her to forgive. She had tried but still felt rejected. I listened for a long time and then prayed with her.

"People in church should act rightly," I said finally, "but only God is always just. Jesus felt rejection too. He understands."

She seemed prepared by the time we reached the church building, but she left the service early, crying. Like someone with a fresh sunburn, it didn't take much for a painful reaction.

I didn't see Anya for ten days. Whenever I went to her apartment, no one answered. We heard she wasn't opening the door to anyone. I finally went to see her at the post office where she worked. She came into the hall by her office to talk to me.

"I haven't seen you for so long..." I began.

"I'm better off alone," she said and began to cry. Her face was twisted with grief and her voice rose in pitch. "I don't want to see anyone—except I have to go to work, so I go. I'm tired of being the scapegoat."

"It's not bad to be alone," I said gently. "Even Jesus needed times alone—as long as you spend it with God." She looked down but didn't say anything. "I love you, Anya. And God loves you too."

We later heard Anya was released from work "on a medical leave" since her depression and constant tears affected her ability to work. Stefan went to see her and had a long talk with her.

Anya came to our house a few days later. "I have a letter that came for you," she said. She had returned to her job at the post office. Still, she didn't look good—a little pale, a little nervous.

"My heart is acting up," she continued. "I wanted to be near a phone in case I need to call an ambulance. Stress makes my heart worse so a doctor gave me permission to stay home from work. I'm back now, but I still feel nervous around people, paranoid. I wonder if I should get psychiatric help."

I'm not one to preach much but I felt a few sermon points building up inside. I got our Russian Bible and asked her read the verses in Philippians 4 about thinking on what is good.

I turned to 2 Corinthians. Paul said he was afflicted but not crushed. "When you are filled up with the love of God," I said, "you won't get crushed when people step on you. Like a box, I can crush it only if it's empty."

We talked for an hour or so, then she said, "My heart is acting normal now. I think I can go home and I'll be all right. Your house has a peaceful spirit. Could we have a Bible study together more often?"

When she came the next day, Anya seemed like her old self again. I shared our leftover potato soup and homemade pizza. She spent the rest of the evening playing with Janelle and Alicia.

Andre, Cory, and Stefan chose eleven men to participate in the church planters training program. They based their decision on recommendations from pastors and their observations of these men. Though most were fairly new Christians, they felt these were the most zealous and had the best potential as church planters.

The leaders invited these prospective students and their wives to two introductory sessions in January. Andre told the group during the first session, "We want you to understand the cost involved before you enter this program. This will be like a full-time job. Your wives must understand too and support you in this undertaking."

The all-day seminar included teaching on God's plan for salvation of the world and why we need new churches. By lunchtime, Cory thought the students felt overwhelmed by the challenge and inadequate to start new churches. In his talk on grace, he said, "God is able to do big things with weak but willing vessels." We had experienced that truth.

Romon, the young pastor from Sudak, taught on marriage. Cory told me later, "I really like Romon. He's only twenty-four, but he has good insights and a fresh style. Andre mentored him. He's read a lot too—Dobson and other books translated into Russian."

The day after this opening seminar, Andre planned to attend a regional council meeting. He faced this meeting with a sense of trepidation. The head of the Baptist Union in Crimea opposed the training program and had rebuked Andre thoroughly on the phone. "I felt like a boy being taken by the ear," Andre told Cory.

"Why haven't you submitted this plan to me and the other brothers?" the head wanted to know.

"I did tell you about it," Andre replied.

"But I didn't think you would really do it."

Cory offered to attend the meeting, but Andre thought he would be treated as a scapegoat. Instead, Andre took the other Russians who would teach in the training program.

Though he expected to get beat up some more, the meeting went well for him. When he told the other leaders about the training center goals, they expressed support and excitement. Some wanted to send students. Others wanted to start something similar in their areas.

The head tried to paint a negative picture: new churches might not follow all the traditions and practices the old churches feel are important. Without support from the council, his arguments fell flat.

These men knew and respected Andre. If Cory, an outsider, had tried to push the program, he probably would not have gained such ready acceptance.

I joined Cory for the second introductory seminar held two weeks later. I wanted to see the church planters, meet their wives, and get a taste of the teaching. Knowing the church in Primorski was very cold in the winter, I wore many layers of clothing. Along with everyone else, I wore my hat and heavy coat the whole time.

Most of the eleven men were in their 20s, but they ranged in age from 21 to 43. Seven were married and four, single. Some wives came, but others stayed home with sick children.

When Cory spoke on "what is a missionary," he reviewed how God chose and used ordinary people. Paul came in weakness, not with clever speech. He talked about what it means to be a bondservant, a slave of God.

During our lunch break, we dined on greasy rice with pickled garlic and green peppers on the side, plus cabbage soup and the all-important bread.

Cory felt very tired that evening, so we went to bed early. Then the phone rang. It was Andre, in Sudak. He had taken some men home, hit icy rain on his way back and couldn't make it over the hill. "Would you drive out and tell my wife I won't be home?" he asked. He had taken three of his children with him and knew his wife would worry.

Cory walked twenty minutes to our garage and fell down on the icy sidewalk. Then he slithered out to Andre's home in a village outside Feodosia. He eventually got to bed again.

Late in January, Anya told me she decided to return to church. She had been away for over a month. "I need to forgive and go on like nothing happened," she said. "I will go to church and greet the brothers." The concept of giving greetings carries much weight in the Russian church culture. Those who have something against another will not greet that person.

On the way to church, Anya told me, "If I knew the brothers accepted me even with makeup, I would stop wearing it." In spite of her lipstick, many people greeted her warmly—but not everyone.

Janelle and Alicia liked playing "Mary and Joseph"

Old women sold sunflower seeds, a common snack food.

A winter storm blew a ship to shore

Our garage was a 20-minute walk away

- 22 -
Training Begins

Andre invited the pastors of Eastern Crimea to attend the February 9th opening session of the training program for church planters. The head of the Crimean Baptist Union had a schedule conflict. Igor said he had to work on his car. Others came, however, and gave their blessing. The pastors from Nizhnigorsk and Primorski thought the teaching was so good, they asked to attend all the sessions.

The group met at the house on the hill where we had lived when we first came to Ukraine. Eleven regular students, plus four teachers and pastors from other towns slept there, "stacked in like cordwood," according to Cory. Cory, Andre, and Stefan went early, before breakfast, and came home late at night.

They met Monday through Thursday, with five lectures each day, plus evening chapel and informal times of fellowship. On Friday morning, Cory finally had time to tell me about his week and the students.

"The fellowship is really good," he said, finishing a leisurely breakfast. "I don't think these guys have had much fellowship with other men. We joke a lot together." He took another sip of coffee. "It's hard to judge how well they're getting the teaching though. They ask many questions trying to process it. I guess that's good."

After the four-day session, the trainees spent the next ten days at home. For homework, they were to review their notes and discuss them with their wives, preach in their home churches, study the book of Acts, and look for and pray for people receptive to the Gospel.

One pastor who sat in on the training program, Piotr, led the church in Primorski, a town near Feodosia. His father was Ivan Mikalovich, the retired pastor of Feodosia. He had his father's gentle spirit, short stature, and love for people. He lacked any formal Bible training, but he wanted to grow and wanted his church members to reach out to others. He asked Cory to preach at his church.

Anya rode with us to Primorski. In this different environment, she was bubbly and outgoing. She volunteered to recite a poem and inspired Janelle and Alicia to sing a Russian song she had taught them.

Twelve teens, most of them new to the church, sat on the stage and provided the special music. A young woman wearing pants and makeup played the violin. Cory gave one of the three sermons, speaking about passing on the grace we have received.

Piotr invited us home after the service. His wife hadn't come to church, so I assumed she was preparing lunch for us. When we got to their apartment, I learned she didn't go to church because she didn't feel well.

I helped her peel potatoes while Cory talked with Piotr and the girls played with their five children. Their apartment didn't have any heat and had water only three brief periods a day. Dirty clothes were piled high in the bathroom. My lot wasn't so bad after all.

After the church planter trainees met again, Andre showed Cory the evaluation forms they had filled out at home. "Do you have some time?" he asked, "I really want you to hear these."

"This is just what we need," wrote one.

"I can't remember when I've had such good fellowship and good food," wrote another. "There's a good mixture of fun and humor along with the serious study."

"I talked to a teacher about some problems and felt accepted."

Many commented on the rich fellowship. One was glad there was no killjoy in the group.

A few said, "We're getting too much information," but most expressed enthusiasm for the whole program.

The main complaint had to do with the heater: some like it hot, some like it cold. "Let's agree on a temperature."

Andre seemed close to tears as he read the evaluations aloud. He had invested much thought and energy in the program and felt encouraged by the positive feedback.

As the week went on, however, it became clear that some struggled with the content of the lectures. The doctrine of salvation by grace contradicted the more legalistic teaching they had heard in their churches. The idea of servant-leadership didn't mesh with their view of a strong leader. Training center leaders pointed to the Bible as the final authority, not church traditions.

The most vocal challenger was a former mafia-member named Pavel. He leaned back in his chair with arms crossed on his chest. He had already started one small group and seemed to think he knew it all. Others imitated his posture.

We had company coming, so I felt motivated for the more unpleasant housekeeping jobs, like washing mildew from windowsills and kitchen walls. We always got a big, black buildup during the winter and I didn't want our apartment to look too slummy when our teammates arrived for a meeting.

Cory came home from his Friday morning walk and said, "There's a little sign on the door downstairs that says, 'Keep your stairwell clean. Because of budget cutbacks no one will clean it for you.'"

I could barely eat my breakfast thinking about a small pile of human waste in the stairwell. It had been there several days. I was used to the smell of stale urine, but I felt like vomiting every time I passed this. Apparently, no one else would clean it up. We had company coming. I added the doo to my to-do list.

Cory scooped up the mess and swept the whole stairwell, an awful undertaking. Jesus washed feet, a demeaning job, and challenged us to do likewise.

All week, Janelle and Alicia had eagerly awaited the arrival of our teammates so they could play with eight-year-old Cameron. I found activities to keep the children busy during our team meeting.

The Wright's ministry in Melitopol had blossomed. Attendance at the Melitopol church was up to 400 adults and 320 children and youth in Sunday School. Church leaders had baptized 39 people the previous year and hoped to build a new sanctuary soon.

We hadn't seen such encouraging results yet, and the question of whether or not we should sign up for another term in Ukraine continued to hang over my head. Cory and I discussed it often.

"I don't like it here most of the time either," he said. "It seems like God is using us though. But I couldn't do it without you. If you don't want to come back, we won't come back. We're in this together."

"I don't know," I said. "We still have a few more months before we have to decide. I guess we'll know when we need to know."

I wrote in my journal:

I can hang on for eighteen more months, but the thought of coming here again feels so depressing. What would we do in the U.S.? I don't know; I just want to be some place where life isn't so hard physically, socially, spiritually, and emotionally. Ultimately, heaven is the only place we will no longer have pain or problems.

Before we came to Ukraine, I told supporting churches, "We have all of eternity to be comfortable. I want my brief life to count for something of eternal value." That is still true—I just want an easier road. What's your perspective, Lord?

"Come unto me, all who are weary and heavy-laden and I will give you rest. Take My yoke upon you and learn from Me, for I am gentle and humble in heart; and you will find rest for your soul. For My yoke is easy, and My load is light."

I come, with burdens of loneliness and sadness. I confess I think your attitude is, "Come to me and I will give you more to carry." But you say, "Come to me when you are carrying too much and I will give you rest." What are we carrying that you don't intend for us to carry? I know we are supposed to be here for now. So what are we not supposed to carry?

Concern for the future and for our health. Anxiety for the welfare of the girls. Concern about our effectiveness. I dump my load at your feet.

Early March brought pleasant weather. When I opened the balcony windows to hang out clothes, we heard the noisy twirping of birds in a nearby tree. Janelle said, "It sounds like Grandma Brown's house."

Spring was my favorite season in Ukraine. Everyone heaved a collective sigh of relief. We survived another winter! Spring brought some windy days and rain, but we saw the sun once again. Gone were the steel-gray skies of winter when icy fog and coal smoke hung over the city for days on end.

Bushes and trees started to show leaves. Old women sold pussy willows at the market for decoration. People began to clean up small flowerbeds in front of some apartments

Janelle and Alicia made a new friend at the playground. Seven-year-old Nadia said, "You be the rabbits and I'll be the wolf." After their game of tag, they floated Styrofoam "boats" on a mud puddle. The girls used sticks to guide their fleet around the miniature lake. Another little girl joined them.

This was the first time Janelle and Alicia played with neighborhood children, so it seemed like a major breakthrough. No longer toddlers, Janelle was six and Alicia, four-and-a-half.

Stefan's eight-year-old daughter Lila was their favorite friend. "Lila smiles at me when she sees me," said Janelle. Lila came to our house for Janelle's birthday and we visited her family. They played hide and seek, ate apples, drew pictures, and did somersaults on a mattress on the floor.

At the next session, Pavel confessed with tears in his eyes, "Men, I've been wrong. What they tell us here is true. We have a lot to learn from them." During the lecture, he leaned forward, taking notes. Others imitated his posture.

As one of five teachers, Cory lectured four to seven hours every other week and prepared more lessons during his free week. Teaching in Russian doubled the challenge.

"Sometimes I feel really inadequate," he told me after one session. "I told Andre and the other teachers, 'I know it is hard to listen to a foreigner speak Russian; I don't have to teach.' They say they can understand me fine though, and recognize I have something to offer. Andre told me, 'These men need to hear new ideas and be challenged in their thinking.'"

When Andre received his training in Moscow, he had a revolutionary breakthrough in his understanding of grace. "Though I'd read about grace in the Bible, I never really understood it before," he told Cory. When teaching basic doctrine, Andre emphasized that we are saved by God's grace, not our works.

One trainee had been divorced and remarried before he became a Christian. The traditional church view was that your real wife is your first wife and any remarriage is adultery. Some Christians told him he should divorce his current wife, also a new Christian, and remarry his first wife, a nonbeliever. He didn't know what he should do and felt great turmoil.

Cory asked the other leaders, "Is divorce an unforgivable sin? Sooner or later we will have to decide this question if we plan to work with nonbelievers."

Andre said, "I've come a long way on my view of this matter. When a woman was caught in adultery, Jesus said, 'He who is without sin, cast the first stone.' And to the woman He said, 'Go and sin no more.'" Jesus gives people a fresh start.

The leaders met with the student, affirmed that God had forgiven him, and encouraged him to move on with his life. This may seem elementary to many Americans, but to the Russian church, it was radical. We heard of a woman who was denied baptism because she had been divorced and remarried three times.

Though funds for the training center came from America, Cory wanted the local leaders to make decisions that were right for the local situation. "I don't want to get in the way," Cory told Andre. "Funds aren't dependent on agreeing with me."

Russians say spring weather is like a woman's temperament—*caprizni* (capricious). We had pleasant sunshine, fierce wind, and drenching rain. One day late in March, it snowed all day.

We needed excitement, so I bundled Janelle and Alicia up and took them out in the blizzard. Few others were out, so we made fresh tracks in the deep snow. I measured about eight inches, more than we had received the whole winter. The girls crawled and rolled and made snow angels.

We walked under trees heavy with snow when a wind shook the branches. "It's an avalanche!" Janelle cried with alarm. Then she made her own "avalanche" by yanking on a branch with Alicia standing under it.

When Cory came home from the training program, he said, "Some of the guys told me that around ten years ago, they got four feet of snow in March and it stayed for two weeks. The whole city was immobilized. Army tanks delivered bread, since nothing else could get through."

National and local elections took place March 29. Walls all around Feodosia held posters promoting various people running for office. One neighbor told me, "I read about one candidate and agree with what he stands for. Then I read about another one and agree with him too. It was easier when we didn't have to choose."

Many people thought the election offered no hope for improving their condition. "They're all bandits," said one person. "They use their position to line their pockets."

The newly elected mayor of Feodosia was either a businessman or in the mafia, depending on whom you talked to. In the minds of some, the terms were identical, since in earlier years it was illegal to make a profit.

Tatiana visited us on April Fool's Day. "Olla will be out of the crib soon and we need to find a bigger place," she said. Options were few and dumpy for those with little money.

"I've been calling on the classified ads in the paper. Today's paper had several houses listed with very low prices. When I called them, people said they didn't have any house for sale. It's because of April Fool's Day. One of my colleagues has been getting calls all day from people wanting to buy a garden plot. She doesn't have a garden plot and didn't place an ad."

During that week's seminar, leaders encouraged church planters to find a "man of peace," someone who might be receptive to the gospel. When Jesus sent out the disciples, He told them to stay with a "man of peace." Though only few may express interest initially, God can use them to draw more people to Christ through their network of relationships.

The students had many questions, "How will I find my man of peace?" "How will I recognize him?" "What should we talk about?"

One student told Cory, "My cousin has asked me to go and do things with him. Do you think I should go?"

Cory asked, "Would it help build your relationship?"

"Yes."

"Then of course you should go." Cory explained that the idea is to build relationships, not blast people with the gospel.

I told Cory, "It seems like a strange question."

He reminded me, "It's reflective of the church culture. You know, 'Be separate from the World.'"

Andre also encouraged the trainees to mentor newer believers. "All your life, you should have someone you are discipling," he said. The goal of the training center was multiplication, not simply addition.

Cory bought produce from roadside stands

Street sweeper

- 23 -
Village Visit

In early April, the girls and I joined Cory on his trip to the village of Nizhnigorsk. He had been there before but this was my first time.

The two-hour drive included miles and miles of farmland between villages. The land belonged to collective farms and included fields of wheat and sugar beets. Large orchards looked like they hadn't been pruned for many years.

A man with a long stick followed fifteen or twenty cows outside one village. I had heard that those who owned cattle in these small towns took turns taking everyone's cattle out to pasture. A woman herded a flock of geese beside the road.

Poplars and other trees lined the road through the steppe. Only stumps remained in some places, as people had cut the windbreak for firewood.

Cory told me about Nizhnigorsk as we drove. "It's also a collective farm village," he said. "The town has only ten or fifteen thousand people, but the church has 150 members." Feodosia's church had fewer members, though the town had some 80,000 residents.

Our first stop was the pastor's house. Right away, I noticed the village smelled different from Feodosia—cleaner, like earth and farm animals. It was quieter too, with little traffic.

I liked their house a lot; it felt homey and peaceful. His wife had decorated their simple home with houseplants and lace curtains. They kept a tidy garden outside. Instead of surrounding their house with grass, they used their soil to grow vegetables, flowers, and fruit. Janelle and Alicia played with a herd of stuffed animals while we drank tea and talked.

Our next stop was Leonid's house. This church planter trainee had been married only three months. His wife, Tamara, had prepared a great feast for us and I joined her in the kitchen.

"How did you meet?" I asked her while slicing bread.

"I used to work with Child Evangelism Fellowship and came to Leonid's village to teach people how to start groups for children." After marriage, she continued to work with children and led two Good News Clubs.

"How many are in each group?" I asked.

"Twenty. Other people lead even more groups in other villages. God has really blessed this work. The children accept Christ, and then their parents start coming to church."

I helped Tamara set food on the table: potatoes with mushrooms, ground chicken patties, pickled tomatoes, and deviled eggs trapped in clear gelatin.

That jello did not impress Janelle and Alicia. "Do I have to eat it?"

Pavel, the oldest church planter, joined us for lunch. A former mafia member, he had a husky build, gray hair, and a life-of-the-party personality. His wife couldn't come, since she had recently given birth to a baby girl and was still in the hospital. They had two adult children and one ten-year-old, so this child was a late addition.

I could tell right away that Pavel loved to tell stories. He told us about his childhood and how he became a Christian. "My father walked out on my mother before I was born," he said. "When I was twelve, my mother left me at Grandma's, since Mama had found another man. I cried every day for my mother."

Pavel became hardened and turned into a hoodlum. When he served in the army, he saw friends die and came to view life as cheap. He wondered, *what is worth living for?* He decided to live for himself.

At the break-up of the Soviet Union, he joined the mafia. It provided a good income, but his wife was unhappy. "There's more to life than this," she told him.

He didn't understand. "What do you mean, 'there's more to life?' I've given you everything you need." She had never told him she came from a Christian family and had turned away from her faith. She wanted to attend church again.

Until he was thirty-six years old, Pavel had never heard about Jesus. He had thirteen crosses for good luck and had occasionally gone to the Orthodox church with his grandma, but he had never heard about Jesus.

Pavel became abusive when he drank. He threw his wife in the car trunk once and bent the trunk when he closed it on her legs. He locked her out of the house several times and made her sleep outside.

Once, in a drunken rage, he tried to choke her. "In Jesus name," she said, "you leave me alone."

He suddenly became weak and came to his senses. He went to bed and slept for twenty-four hours. Not long afterward, he gave his life to Christ.

Almost six years had passed since he repented. When he left the mafia, he received several threats, but nothing happened to him. He remained in contact with some mafia members. One told him, "It's good you got out six years ago when you did. I want to get out, but I can't."

I was surprised to hear of mafia in such a small village—but even American grade schools have bullies who beat up classmates that don't hand over their lunch money.

Pavel started a "tea and cookies" outreach to nonbelievers in a village about fifteen miles from his. He didn't say anything about church initially; he just invited people he met on the street to a believer's house for tea. He wired the house lights to a car battery since the electricity was off in the evening. His wife accompanied him, and they began to sing.

Passersby, seeing the light and hearing singing, figured there must be a party and came for free vodka. After several had gathered, he read a few verses from the Bible without making any comment. They served tea with cookies and everyone talked informally. After tea, Pavel asked if anyone had questions about the scripture he had read. The following discussion often went until midnight. The group had grown to twenty members, and fifteen had accepted Christ.

Along with the other church planters, Pavel knew he must start a new group. He considered his own village as a target region, but this idea made him nervous. "Too many people there know me," he said with a big grin.

I helped Tamara clear the table and she got out their photo album. She showed a picture of the Nizhnigorsk church youth group with around thirty or more teenagers. Most came from non-Christian homes, she explained, and many parents followed them in church attendance. Thirty people were preparing for baptism that summer, when the water was warmer.

While we talked, Janelle and Alicia played outside. They fed bones to the dog, gathered chicken feathers, and climbed a tree. The weather was perfect, for early April.

On our way home, we passed a bus pulled over near a clump of brush and trees. People streamed from the bus and disappeared into the trees, a Ukrainian rest stop.

All winter, I had anticipated the arrival of my sister, Linda, and her husband, Mike, who hoped to adopt two little boys from Ukraine. We wrote often over e-mail to discuss adoption details, and I arranged for people to help them with the process.

While waiting for their train in Simferopol, I saw several street kids, around ten years old, sniffing glue from plastic bags. A missionary who worked with such street kids told me that many of them earned money for glue through prostitution. Many children who grow up in state-run "orphanages," end up on the street when they are old enough to run away.

Mike and Linda obtained permission to adopt from a large children's home in Simferopol, the capitol of Crimea. Few children there were actually orphans—typically, their mothers abandoned them at maternity hospitals at birth.

Janelle and Alicia were excited to see their aunt and uncle but wished their cousins might have come too. We stayed together in Simferopol for much of April in an apartment obtained for a missionary family who had not yet arrived. On our visits to the children's home on the edge of town, the girls liked playing at the playground, set in pine trees. "It smells like Grandma Brown's here," they said.

Mike and Linda chose two little boys, ages six months and ten months, named Nicholi and Eliya. Foreigners could not adopt perfectly healthy children, but these two simply had irregular heartbeats.

The adoption process was a lengthy ordeal. After standing in lines all day one day without accomplishing anything, they came home feeling very discouraged and frustrated with the system. The smells of the crowd plus the sense of despair, hostility, and oppression seemed overwhelming.

"You just want to get out of there, and you don't care what else happens," said Mike.

I understood. We also had experienced the sense of "what did we get ourselves into." On the positive side, when feeling helpless we came to realize that if anything good ever did happen, God must get all the credit.

Eventually, they successfully adopted the boys and renamed them Nicholas and Elliott. Locals spoke with respect for Linda when they learned she adopted two children, especially since she already had three at home. Few modern couples in Ukraine had more than one child. "She is so brave," they said.

Linda told me, "I'm not brave, just greedy." She had always wanted a large family.

While the girls and I hosted Mike and Linda, Cory continued his work with the church planters. The leaders thought they had chosen men with the best potential, but they still encountered problems. Some participants equated salvation with adherence to church traditions and struggled with the doctrine of grace. Some doubted God wanted Christians to start new churches.

Andre explained it to Cory, "The older Baptist churches have rules against anyone speaking about founding a new church." It was a way to avoid church splits. He gave students examples from the Bible how the Gospel spread through new church plants.

Many trainees spent their free week working with their home church—since it was easier—instead of trying to start new churches.

Andre told them, "You need to keep a journal. Set ministry goals each week and analyze how you spend your time. In making plans and in your evaluation, you need to ask yourself, 'How will this help me to plant a new church?'"

Even after all trainees had identified a "man of peace," most still struggled with the next step: getting a small group started. We decided that if only half of the men ended up starting a cell group, we could call the program a success.

One of the students didn't come to a training session late in May, so Andre went to find out why. The young man was very hostile. He said the program was dumb, the teachers were stupid, the students were stupid too, and he wasn't coming back. He accused Andre of being in it for the money, of being a puppet of the West.

Andre had taken this young man under his wing and had helped him financially and spiritually for several years—so the conversation was very unpleasant. Moreover, Andre had taken a pay-cut to lead this program, and he had wanted to train church planters long before Western help made it possible.

Cory told me, "This guy used to complain a lot about the homework and hardly ever did it."

I commented, "It's easier to say, 'the program is stupid,' instead of admitting, 'I can't fulfill the expectations of the program.'"

"He has been visiting Igor a lot the last few weeks, and you know what Igor thinks. He also lives with his mother who is into the occult and tells fortunes. Andre told me, 'He's living in a house with demons.'"

After this negative report, Cory wondered what the other trainees thought about the program. He decided to ask the men he mentored on his next trip to Nizhnigorsk.

The girls and I joined Cory on his visit to the village. The women and children got together at one house, while Cory and the men talked at another house. I asked Tamara, Leonid's wife, how Leonid liked his training so far.

"He likes it very well," she said. "It's so practical, like the idea of building relationships with nonbelievers and discipling new Christians. Usually, we just expect people to come to church and repent. If they fall away, then we say, 'Well, he wasn't a genuine Christian in the first place.'"

On our drive home, Cory told me, "I'm really encouraged. They asked many good questions and they are planning how to start new churches. They've grown a lot and they're enthusiastic about the training program."

As we drove, we saw people from villages gathering grass for hay along the road. They cut the tall grass with a scythe and then piled it on a horse-drawn wagon or a person-drawn cart.

Cory commented, "The people who work at collective farms aren't getting their salaries either." They survived by growing their own produce and raising animals.

Two weeks later, Cory visited the church planters in Nizhnigorsk again and attended the Bible study Pavel had started a year earlier. Over twenty people had already accepted Christ through this group.

They began at 7:00 with cake and tea, held a Bible study from 8:30 to 9:30, and then sang for an hour. Group members filled the living room of the house where they met with an over-flow crowd in the kitchen.

The scripture passage they covered included a verse that mentioned stealing. Pavel asked the group, "Does that mean when you are milking cows for the collective farm you shouldn't take home a jar for yourself?" Such pilfering was common.

Cory was impressed with the joyful atmosphere and the skill with which Pavel led the study. "I don't think I could lead it that effectively," he told me later. "I don't know the culture as well as he does."

- 24 -
Camp and the KGB

Mid-June, Tatiana called us and announced, "We bought the flat to-day!" She and her husband, Victor, had been looking for low-cost housing for months.

In May, they had found a suitable apartment in their price range. The woman selling it said she needed some money to get all the papers ready and if they were serious, they should give her $200 for a down payment.

After a few weeks, it became clear that the woman did not intend to sell them the apartment and would not return their money. "Someone stole the money and my identification papers," she said. "I can't sell without my documents, and I have no money to give you."

Tatiana and Victor spent many hours waiting for her outside her house. Many other angry people came to pound on her door, demanding their money back. These had also given her a down payment.

Tatiana and Victor finally got the phone number of a businessman who had the papers to her apartment in his safe. He had the papers since the woman had not paid him the total amount for the apartment. He put pressure on the woman, and she finally followed through with the sale.

"Our meeting at the notary office today was awful," Tatiana said. "The woman was crying with tears, saying, 'These people are forcing me out of my house.'" Victor and the businessman shouted at her, but that was the only way she would sign the papers.

We had two summer interns again who came to work with English-speaking students. In honor of Fourth of July, we took them to the woods for a hot dog roast and picnic. We drove just ten minutes out of town, then up a hill on a rutted dirt road. Cory had been to this spot before with the youth group, but it was my first time.

The grove was tiny compared to Oregon's forests, but I loved the pine smell, the sound of birds, and the crunch of pine needles underfoot. The girls said they liked hearing the wind as it blew through the trees. They scampered to gather sticks for their first hot dog roast. We picked wildflowers on a grassy hill overlooking the sea for a brilliant bouquet to take home as a reminder of our outing.

Though Feodosia was supposed to be a tourist resort, I disliked the smells of diesel exhaust and garbage, the dirt, the crowds, and noise. By this, our third summer in Ukraine, we finally found a few get-away spots. Another day, Cory took us up the coast to a beach with fewer people and cleaner water.

In July, two American teams came to help with two different day camps. These groups brought craft supplies, sports equipment, and enthusiasm.

Around 100 children came for the first camp. We expected about 80 the second week but ended up with 167! Many of the extras came because of the interns' contacts with Lingua Club, an English language institute.

The team covering that week said they had prayed they would have as many children as they could handle. They brought extra supplies and had enough. Most children attending came from non-churched backgrounds. For many, it was their first time to learn about the Bible.

Later in the week, I talked to an older woman who came to get her granddaughter. She had tears in her eyes as she told me, "Thank you, thank you so much for having this camp. My granddaughter likes it so much. She is happy. She sings songs at home that she has been learning. She had a cough last night, so I told her she couldn't come today, but she cried and begged, 'Please let me go to camp. I won't go swimming today, just let me go, please.'"

The next day, this woman gave a letter to a camp worker. It read:

Three days ago, I didn't believe there is anywhere on earth any goodness or unselfishness. There is a lot of corruption, evil, and lies, and sometimes you feel you don't want to live anymore.

I am already an old and useless woman, but it is very painful to look at children who have known neither kindness nor warmth. I am afraid for their future. It doesn't matter that old people are forgotten—we are sinners and deserve it—but we can't forget about our children.

Thanks to you, our children believe there is still goodness and joy. May God give you strength, patience, and happiness. May God always be with you, in your kind hearts. Pray for us.

With sincere respect,
Grandmother Zoya

The next Sunday in church, I noticed a blond woman with makeup and no head covering and made a point of talking to her after the service. "How did you find out about this church?" I asked.

She had been studying English at Lingua club and had met various visitors we'd had from America who visited her class. "The songs and the church service touched me deeply," she said, "Is my makeup smeared from crying?" Fortunately, she came during a service without sermons against makeup.

We had lunch that day with the American team and their hostess, Ludmila. She said she wanted to talk to Igor about the makeup issue but wasn't sure how.

"I share my faith with many nonbelievers," she said. "Sometimes I invite them to church, but when I hear sermons about external appearance, I'm glad they don't come. God looks on the heart. You can look plain outside, but that doesn't change your heart. Our goal is supposed to be to reach people for Christ, not insulate ourselves from the world."

The day before, three new believers from Feodosia had been baptized in the Black Sea, the total number for the year. "It's too bad there weren't more," Ludmila said, "but people need to feel loved and accepted first." The pastor of a tiny church in Kirovskaya, a church planter, had baptized nine during the same service.

Anya and Vladimir Alexandrovich, the thin old man with black glasses and a warm smile, got tired of waiting for Cory and Andre to start a new church in Feodosia and decided to start their own Bible study for nonbelievers. Cory and Andre didn't have time to start a group in Feodosia and knew it would face fierce opposition.

Anya and Vladimir had met twice with several others when Igor called a members' meeting at the church.

"I understand there is a new church meeting in the home of Anya Mikalovna being led by Vladimir Alexandrovich," he said. "These two are going against the Word of God. No one sent them out and no one laid hands on them. If they continue, they will be excommunicated, and I don't want to hear that any of you are attending their meetings."

Vladimir decided he could not afford to continue. His wife was bedridden after a series of strokes and he needed other women in the church to help care for her.

Janelle and Alicia looked forward to my birthday more than I did. They made paper chains two weeks early, saying, "We need to decorate." Then they worked on cards and party hats. Alicia told me, "We want your birthday to be your *best* birthday ever, because you are our mommy and you take care of us."

Her enthusiastic affection brought tears to my eyes and I thought, *God wants us to be like that...like children.* God delights in those who can lay aside their "give-me" list and say, "I want to give You my *best*, because You are my Daddy and You take care of me."

The girls eagerly gave me their gifts after our dinner at Anya's house. They presented me with a paper airplane with pictures drawn on it. "That's you and me and Sissy," Alicia said.

Next I unwrapped an empty plastic container that once held candy. "You can put small garbage in it," said Janelle. "I put a fish sticker on it because you like to swim."

I received a hair band, and then a piece of cardboard with sparkly crayon scribbled on it. "The sparkles are fireworks," Janelle explained.

They also helped Daddy pick out a coffee mug and some roses, but their original gifts seemed more precious. I didn't know what I'd do with a paper airplane or sparkly cardboard but appreciated the love behind them.

God doesn't need our gifts to keep Him in business, I realized. After all, He owns the cattle on a thousand hills and created galaxies by His word. Still, He delights in meager offerings given from a grateful heart.

August weather had turned hot and humid, with daytime temperatures reaching 95 degrees and it didn't drop below 80 at night. Inside, it stayed in the high 80s both day and night. Without air conditioning, I kept cool by taking a dip in our bathtub several times a day. We slept without sheets but still woke up sweating. We heard it was 110 degrees inland. When Cory drove to other villages, he said it felt like he was driving on ice, since the pavement was melting.

Because of the heat, training sessions with the church planters started at 5:00 a.m. The students usually took naps in the afternoon, but Cory's meetings and other activities resulted in long days. He came home around 10:00 p.m.

Many members of the first cell-group Pavel had started were sharing their faith with others. Their village sponsored an event every Sunday afternoon called "Harmony." Participants typically sang sad folk songs or recited poetry.

Several in Pavel's Bible Study group went and asked to sing. After a solo, a duet, and a few group numbers, they noticed the person in charge seemed upset by this religious music, so they finished and sat down. The audience clapped enthusiastically and many came to tell them how much they liked their joyful music. A few days later, the person in charge also complimented them on how well they sang and invited them to sing again.

On Cory's next visit to Nizhnigorsk, he spent the night at Leonid's home, whose wife was expecting her first baby. Leonid had asked Cory if we had any chalk she could eat, for calcium, since she didn't like to drink milk. Cory took her my pudding recipe and some prenatal supplements.

For breakfast, she served him fried potatoes and salad, fried pig fat (guess that's better than raw pig fat), fried eggplant, and fried bread. For some reason, he wasn't hungry for lunch when he got home.

The intelligence office, formerly known as the KGB, wanted to meet with Stefan. Several weeks earlier, they called on Igor and asked him about the children's camp and training center. He told them to talk to Stefan, so they went to the church on a weekday and left a message for Stefan to go to the KGB office on a certain day.

Stefan called the office and told them that he couldn't meet with them on that day and if they want to see him, they could come to the church to talk to him. "I am here every Sunday morning."

He told Cory, "I know their tactics. They like to get you alone in an office."

Several weeks went by and they didn't come. We heard they visited Primorski and questioned several people about the American visitors who had been there. Then they called on some people living next to the old church property, where the training sessions took place, and asked about the activity next door. The neighbor said, "They are teaching the Bible."

They called on Stefan again and he arranged to meet them at the church. He came to our house after the meeting and told us about it. The agent had asked him about the camp. "What do you teach the children?"

Stefan replied, "We teach from the Bible. We are concerned about the moral decline in the country and want these children to live correctly."

The man asked about the training center. Stefan again said, "We teach about the Bible."

He asked about the American visitors we have had. Stefan said, "They came to help with the camp and bring supplies. We don't have the things necessary for running a camp."

He asked about us, how long we had lived there and what we did. Stefan responded, "They have been here three years and they teach the Bible." Stefan told us, "They already know how long you have been here. They have your visa records."

Stefan asked him, "May I ask why you are asking these questions?"

He responded that he was looking to see if anyone had broken any laws and was surprised no one had.

We found this interest from the KGB unnerving, having grown up with more freedom and privacy. One person told us, "I'm one hundred percent sure the KGB listens to your phone conversations." We heard from other Americans in Crimea that their e-mail was not secure.

Though we thought of ourselves as ordinary folk, we were the only foreigners in town. Apparently, they were suspicious of our motives. We had heard that some people thought we were spies—why else would Americans come to this backwater town with poor living conditions?

If times got tough again, we could always leave, but we felt concern for our friends. We had heard that a KGB agent threatened a Christian in another town, "You are free now, but we have a file that thick on all of you. When the time is right, we'll use it."

Our friends didn't expect freedom of religion to continue but used this window of opportunity to spread the Gospel.

- 25 -
"Blessed Inconveniences"

For Anya's birthday, in late August, we took her to the patch of trees on the hill for fresh air and a hot dog roast. I also wanted to pick blackberries since I'd seen berry bushes there during our Fourth of July outing.

I optimistically took many containers, but someone more eager had already been there. Nevertheless, while munching unripe berries, Janelle and Alicia declared it was the "best birthday party."

Anya thought so too. She had never roasted hot dogs before or visited this "forest." While we searched for berries, Anya said, "God has blessed me so much. You are my friends. If you weren't here, I would have left the church. Now I have a ministry with the children in Batalnaya."

I had heard about this collective farm village. For over a year, Stefan had been leading Saturday and Sunday services at a new church there. Vladimir Alexandrovich, who helped him occasionally, said the services were "like a breath of fresh air," since the newer believers were so eager to learn and grow.

Around fifteen to twenty adults usually attended the church. During a vigorous calling program that summer, many people in the village said they weren't interested in attending but promised to send their children. A visiting American team held a children's program and after they left, Stefan asked Anya to teach Sunday school.

"Those children are so loving," Anya said. "They run up and hug me when they see me."

"They love you because you love them," I replied. "You are gifted to work with children. I could never do it as well as you."

She popped another berry in her mouth. "The people in that church don't care if I wear makeup or not. They are all new believers. After working in the fields all week, they like to dress up on Sunday too; it's like a holiday for them."

The previous week, about fifteen children came to Anya's class and ranged in age from five to fourteen. "The village children are so much easier to work with than children in the city," she said. "The stories are new to them and they are polite. They love to color, even the older ones. They don't have crayons at home, since crayons aren't Russian."

The church in Primorski had started the Batalnaya church with the help of an American team. The Primorski pastor, Piotr, continued to attend our training program and again asked Cory to come and preach.

I liked the atmosphere at this church, and I saw new faces—many with makeup on. Attendance was up to eighty people compared to fifty during our previous visit in the spring, even with the youth group gone to help with an evangelistic outreach in another town.

September brought crisp mornings followed by warm sunshine, like the back-to-school days of my childhood. Janelle, officially in first grade, and Alicia, in kindergarten, had very different approaches to learning. Janelle eagerly filled out page after page in her workbook. Alicia took the creative approach and needed more prodding to keep on task.

"Look Mama!" she'd say, "These X's are doing jumping jacks. They are holding hands and touching feet…. Look Mama! This 'S' is a swan." She had drawn a head and tail feathers. "School is more fun when I make funny pictures," she added.

The girls had little friends in our courtyard. They drew with chalky rocks and played tag. One little boy let himself get caught and the girls led him all over, holding his hands.

"What an obedient boy!" observed Anya as we watched them play.

Though playground equipment was minimal, the children found other ways to pass the time. One day, they decorated a bush with candy wrappers, plastic cola bottles, and other trash.

"Look Mama!" Janelle said, "We made a Christmas tree!"

They jumped on the springs of an easy chair that had disintegrated long ago. The cement leg of a broken bench made a good teeter-totter when balanced on a rock. Broken bottles worked great when digging for hidden treasure—until Mama came on the scene.

They showed me a pile of used syringes other children had collected. "I hope you didn't touch those," I said. "Did you?" They shook their heads.

Cory continued to meet with the church planters every other week and brought home news of their progress. The man who had dropped out of the program in May came to Andre and apologized. He said he had made a big mistake and asked if he could come back.

Cory and Stefan also met with him to discern his motives. The leaders decided to accept him back with a two-month probation. He had continued building relationships with nonbelievers during his absence and said it was the one thing that gave him a sense of purpose.

Leaders had hoped all the church planters would have groups started by that summer but few met this goal. The leaders prayed and discussed ways to tighten accountability. They felt they could not give the students all the support they needed and decided the men from each region should form their own accountability groups. They could pray together and encourage each other.

That still wasn't enough. Cory came home frustrated after the first day of the next session. "They're acting like a bunch of children," he said. "They complain about the homework. A lot of them just don't hand any in. It was the same way this morning. The ones who are married blame their wives for demands on their time."

The leaders prayed some more and then gave several sermons on topics like personal integrity and the fact that we will all give account to God. They believed that if the men would simply put in eight hours a day toward getting a new group started, they would be successful.

Andre reminded them that they had all signed a contract agreeing to devote eight hours a day toward church planting; and their wives signed, showing their support. They received a stipend so they could be free to devote that much time. He told them to start recording how much time they put in each day. If they worked only half time, they could expect half their stipend.

Cory told me the response from the men was unexpectedly positive. Several said, "We need this kind of accountability" and "I wish you had started this in the beginning."

Even Jesus put up with immaturity in the group He chose—yet most turned out all right in the end. We hoped our group would too.

Anya lost her job at the post office. She tended to speak her mind and stand up for what she thought was right; not everyone appreciated it. Angered by her boss's unjust treatment, she took her case to court, certain of a win. Though co-workers privately cheered for her, no one would speak on her behalf. She lost the case.

"It's better this way," she told me later. "I don't have to spend my spend my days in that oppressive atmosphere."

Since she was free, I recruited her to help me put up new wallpaper in my kitchen. The old paper had turned black from mildew, and in many places it had fallen off the wall. She welcomed the project and I welcomed her help.

I also asked her to help teach the girls more Russian. She taught them Bible verses and songs. She sat with them in the courtyard where they could hear Russian and practice it with neighborhood children.

A new teammate arrived late in September. June Johnson had come to Feodosia two years earlier for ten days to help with a camp. During that visit, she got bit with the missions bug and her life changed forever. The nursing job she once loved became unsatisfying. She applied to our mission organization, quit her job, sold her house, and came to join us. What drives people to such insanity?

June moved in with Ludmila, a woman in the Feodosia church with an apartment bigger than most and a telephone. Short-term teams from America had often stayed in Ludmila's home.

June planned to spend the first six months of her two-year term focusing on learning Russian and then work in a clinic at the Primorski church. Americans had helped build the clinic behind the church and teams had come for medical outreach in the community several summers in a row. A Russian Christian doctor worked at the clinic.

When I'd first met June eight years earlier, I noticed her warm smile and confident demeanor. Not until later did I realize she walked with a limp and had one shoe with an extra thick sole.

As I got to know her better, she explained she had been born with multiple congenital problems of unknown cause. She needed immediate surgery after birth so she could eat without fluids going into her lungs. Eleven more corrective surgeries followed over the next twenty years to correct clubfoot, scoliosis, and bowel and bladder problems.

"When I was in second grade," she said, "I began to realize I was different from the other kids. In fourth or fifth grade, I started to feel self-conscious around others and angry with God. I remember sobbing, shaking my fist at Him and asking, 'Why did You do this to me?!' I hated Him. Later, a youth pastor helped me see I could be friends with God."

Having spent much time in the hospital, June decided at a young age she wanted to be a nurse. She reached her goal and grew in her relationship with the Lord and acceptance of her condition. "I began to see my physical problems as a gift from God," she said, "since I could relate to my patients in a way others could not."

June was like Mary Poppins to Janelle and Alicia. She read to them, played games, and talked to them like they were people. Making them feel special seemed to come naturally to her. I enjoyed her companionship too.

A few weeks after her arrival, June and I took the train to Kiev to attend a women's conference. About 180 women attended: missionaries and a few English-speaking Ukrainian women. June and I shared a room together at our conference spot in a forest outside Kiev.

The featured speaker, Elizabeth Elliot, gave convicting and challenging messages. She became a widow as a young missionary when Auca Indians killed her husband. Though she had been through tough times, she never encouraged self-pity. Her meaty talks helped me more than if she had said, "You poor dears, I know just how you feel."

She spoke on the value and necessity of suffering. "If Christ, our Lord, suffered, why should we expect anything different?" She defined suffering as "having what you don't want or wanting what you don't have." Hard times help shape our character, she said, to make us more like Christ. God makes all things work together for good if we give our difficulties to Him. In acceptance, there is peace.

She talked about "blessed inconveniences." After that session, a leader asked us to tell someone nearby about something we found difficult. I thought of how people used the entryway to our apartment building as a toilet. I was used to the urine smell but we got a more solid "present" the previous week. I finally cleaned it up, since it didn't go away by wishful thinking.

"Now," the leader said, "Thank God for your area of difficulty."

Could I be truly thankful for this? I *could* be thankful that Jesus left a perfectly pure and clean realm to live in a polluted world.

In another session, Elizabeth Elliot told the story of a woman who dealt with a series of difficulties, including the sickness and death of her mother. The stress could have crushed her but with each new crisis, she continued to say, "For this, I have Jesus."

When we returned to Feodosia, I found another "blessed inconvenience" in the entryway. I took our garbage pail and a piece of thin cardboard down the stairs, trying to be grateful for the opportunity to serve my neighbors. *For this, I have Jesus.*

Our picnic spot on a hill overlooking the Black Sea

June Johnson joined us, focusing on medical ministry

- 26 -
If You Don't Lose Heart

By late-October, the church planters had started five new groups. One of them told Cory, "The accountability helps us break bad habits." An American ministry once sponsored him to plant a church. "But they gave us no guidance and no one checked on us. They wanted us to send a report, but they paid us even if we didn't do anything."

Pavel needed no prodding, however. Cory came home encouraged after visiting a new group Pavel started in another collective farm village. The collective farm was the primary source of employment for most villages in the area and typically, the boss was the most powerful man in town. In some ways, life hadn't changed much since the feudal system, when peasants worked for a powerful landowner.

Pavel went to the boss and told him he wanted to start a Bible study for the people of the village. The man didn't like the idea.

"Do you like having your workers steal from you?" Pavel asked.

"Well, no."

Pavel explained he wanted to build moral character and make a better society. "You try to prevent stealing in your way," he said, "and I will work on it from the spiritual side."

The boss agreed and even gave Pavel a large room where they could hold the Bible study. They started with just a few people, but after three weeks, sixty came. Pavel said he could already see five men who had the potential to be future leaders—one was a believer already and the others showed keen interest in spiritual things.

The group Pavel had started a year and a half earlier was so big it needed to be split into two groups. He recognized he had made the mistake of not preparing it for multiplication from the beginning. In the training program, he learned it's not enough to start a new group; he must train others to take on positions of leadership.

"Pavel's wife really wants to meet you," Cory told me when he got home. The last time I had been to Nizhnigorsk, Vera was still recovering from delivering their child. So early in November, the girls and I joined Cory on his next trip to this village.

After we arrived at Pavel's house, he led me to the "summer kitchen," a shed behind the house where Vera was making dinner. His wife was short but sturdy, like most Russian women. She greeted me warmly, then continued to work.

She spooned a dab of mashed potatoes on a flattened piece of dough, wrapped the dough around, and pinched the edges together. It didn't look too hard, so I helped her assemble the vereneki. Flies buzzed around us while we talked.

"It was a miracle when my husband came to the Lord," she said. "And now he is telling others about Christ. Oh, our life was terrible when we didn't follow God. I'm from a Christian family, but I didn't accept Christ until I was thirty-two. I came to the place where I wanted to kill myself. Pavel was in the mafia and harsh. I put my face in a pillow one day, cried and cried...and Jesus met me there. He changed my life. Then my husband came to Christ. God is so good."

She put some vereneki into a pot of boiling water on the stove, then returned to the small table to make more. "God has blessed Pavel's ministry and the group he started has really grown. Oh, these new believers love to sing."

Vera burst into song, turning her humble summer kitchen into a sacred place. I liked her and her bubbly personality. Most women in Ukraine were reserved: sad, serious, self-conscious, or suspicious. Vera was different.

We brought the cooked vereneki to the main house and found Janelle and Alicia playing catch with an eleven-year-old boy with sparkling eyes and an easy grin. Pavel and Vera also had a 22-year-old son and a 21-year-old daughter, who lived away from home, and a seven-month-old baby girl. The baby had bright eyes and a sweet smile.

After we ate, Vera picked up her little girl and told me, "The doctors thought I should abort this baby. They said I was too old to have children. They think thirty is too old, and I'm forty-two."

I knew most couples in Ukraine had only one child and had heard that the most common form of birth control was abortion.

"I couldn't have an abortion though," she continued. "Abortion is murder, a sin. I have been down that road before, and I felt so bad, even when I wasn't a Christian."

When Vera went in for delivery, a nurse mocked her for wanting to give birth at an old age. "What, is this your second life?" she asked. "Were you born again?"

In fact, yes. Several people listened as Vera gave her testimony.

Pavel said that an English teacher in a neighboring village wanted to meet us, so we all drove to her apartment. This classy-looking woman with perfect makeup and hairdo had prepared a large meal for us featuring "blini," thin pancakes. Some blini she filled with cottage cheese, others with hamburger.

While we sipped tea after dinner, she persuaded her older son to play a couple pieces on the piano. Her younger son refused to sing.

"I know many of Shakespeare's sonnets," she told us. "Shall I recite some Shakespeare for you?" She recited. "Do you like classical music? Shall I play some Beethoven for you?" She played.

She must have been a nervous wreck trying to figure out how to feed and entertain these Americans properly. If America were Russia, we would have been peasants, but she treated us like diplomats.

Though she had planned to do postgraduate work in Moscow on "English verbs of action," she got married instead to an agronomist and moved to a collective farm village. So this woman of culture was stuck in a village trying to teach young people who lacked motivation to learn and wasn't getting paid for it.

"Some teachers are going to work in the market," she said. "But I cannot do that. I am not a peddler, I am a teacher." She started attending church services and said she felt emotionally moved during the meeting, especially by the singing.

Not long after our visit, she accepted Christ and began playing the piano for church services.

Our new teammate, June, spent every Sunday afternoon at our home. We all looked forward to this time together.

"How did your week go?" I asked her during lunch.

"I got a cold," she said, "and Ludmila is sure it's because the kitchen window had been left open. It makes me wonder how I will fit in here. People have such different ideas about sickness and medicine."

She sipped her coffee and continued, "I don't want to work in competition or opposition to local doctors and nurses, but I can't practice medicine at a level lower than what I know is right. You came here with some very different ideas about evangelism. How did you do it?"

"We waited until we found people we could work with," I said, "people with a similar vision. I think you will find others who will welcome what you have to offer."

Some American churches had sent the Primorski church clinic a container full of American medicines and medical supplies. The goods were needed, but the Russian doctor wasn't sure how to use many of them. June went to the clinic with Tatiana to help the doctor sort and figure out what was what.

While she was there, a well-known fortuneteller came in. The woman had lost much weight from complications after an operation. The doctor asked June to look at the woman's infected wound, since June was a wound specialist.

The doctor told the woman she needed to get her life right spiritually and urged her to get rid of her fortune-telling cards and other things related to the occult. Before she left, the woman prayed—confessed her sin and asked God for forgiveness.

June continued to learn Russian and began going to the clinic once a week. She worked to get information about American medicines translated into Russian with Tatiana translating and Anya typing.

When it snowed and cold weather hit later in November, wintertime electricity rationing also began. The city (and country) didn't have enough electricity to supply everyone's needs. Our power was typically off four hours or more each day.

I went two weeks without washing clothes—waiting for a day with electricity, water, and no rain. I was glad I hadn't chopped all the elastic off Cory's extra underwear since it looked like I'd be wearing his soon.

Then Alicia called out around 3:00 a.m. "MOMMY! MY THROAT HURTS!"

I gave her a drink and told her, "Screaming like that won't help anything."

Fifteen minutes later: "IT STILL HURTS!"

I tended to her again and finally got back to sleep.

"MOMMY, I'M GOING TO THROW UP!"

I dashed to the kitchen for a bowl, but by the time I reached her, it was too late. Two more episodes got two pillows and her bedding.

I couldn't wash clothes or blankets the next morning since the water was off. Elizabeth Elliot said, "In acceptance there is peace." And there was.

Power outages became more severe—up to ten hours during the day and more at night. I got increasingly cranky one day when I wanted to work on the computer and the electricity didn't come on when I thought it should. A trip to the market helped. Seeing all those people standing in below-freezing weather trying to make a living, I knew I had it easy.

Have you thought more about whether or not we should come back to Ukraine after our furlough?" Cory asked.

We had given ourselves until the end of the year to make a decision. I hadn't forgotten.

"What are you thinking?" I replied.

"Sometimes I just want to go home, but I feel like we are able to help here in ways we can't in the U.S. But I know it's hard for you here and I don't want to stay if you don't."

One year had passed since my friend Vicky said, "You can't make a decision based on whether or not something is hard." I had replayed her words many times.

I later read the verse, "Let us not lose heart in doing good, for in due time we shall reap if we do not grow weary" (Gal. 6:9). It challenged me toward perseverance. I didn't want to give up too soon and miss seeing the results of our labor.

While wrestling with the decision, I thought of the horses we had on the farm while I was growing up. When I broke a young filly, she would jerk on the rope, shake her head, and run in circles. I had been like that horse. Resisting takes a lot of energy. Life is easier when walking submissively, letting God take the lead.

"No, it's not an easy place to live," I told Cory, "but I am able to live here. I guess I feel like we're supposed to come back too."

After I stopped fighting with God, life in Ukraine became more enjoyable. Sure, our water and electricity continued to go off, and our entryway still smelled like an outhouse, but I stopped looking for things to justify my discontent.

Eleven church planters received training

They took time out for fellowship

- 27 -
Graduation

For over ten months, the church planters had met every other week for teaching and discussion. When they gathered for their final session late in November, they reviewed highlights of their training. Several said they liked the fellowship the best.

One said, "I wanted to reach out to nonbelievers before, but I didn't know how. This training has given me better direction and tools for the task."

A couple men commented on the marriage and family teaching. "I thought it was the man's job to rule and learned that I need to serve my wife."

"I've learned about humility. I see how our leaders work as a team and one person doesn't try to dominate. I realized I don't have to always get my own way."

"I felt that I was always dealing with the sins in my past and this has helped me get beyond them."

"I always thought the verse in the Bible about 'brothers dwelling together in unity' was ironic, but now, I know it really can happen."

Several said they learned self-discipline and how to budget their time.

Cory came to get June and me to take us to the graduation ceremony at the Primorski church that evening. Though the town of Primorski sat in darkness, light shone from the church windows. Stefan had petitioned the town authorities to give us electricity for this special occasion.

The church planters had invited their wives, if married, and parents, if single, for the graduation program and a special meal afterward. Several church leaders also attended.

The head of the Crimean Baptist Union came. He had been opposed to the training program until Alexi asked him to sign the diplomas and speak.

Though Igor didn't come, several brothers from Feodosia church did. They shook Cory's hand and voiced their support. Feodosia's youth choir provided special music and presented several skits. Two church planters sang a funny song they had made up about the leaders and the program.

The cooks served mashed potatoes, meat loaf patties, and cabbage salad. It was Thanksgiving Day in America. Though we lacked the traditional turkey, we felt grateful for all God had done in the lives of these men. Five had started small groups and we hoped the rest would also find success.

One month later, the church planters gathered for an all-day meeting, part of their ongoing mentoring. Andre and Cory taught, and the men gave updates on their work.

Sergei and Leonid, of Nizhnigorsk, had written a series of four tracts for distribution at five hundred apartment buildings in town. These tracts spoke to the Russian soul better than tracts translated from English.

Leonid said that when they started giving out the first set of tracts he felt very nervous. No one slammed the door in his face, however, and residents seemed interested. When they went back later with the second in the series, people welcomed them warmly.

Sergei had been ordained that month as the new pastor of the Nizhnigorsk church since the former pastor emigrated to the U.S. Besides continuing with door-to-door evangelism, he hoped to mobilize the congregation to plant more churches in the surrounding area. The church, already outreach-oriented, had added forty-six people that year through baptism.

Some church planters held an art exhibit of Christian paintings. Hundreds of people attended the exhibit and heard the stories behind the paintings. Some showed Christian films in homes and theaters and evangelized door-to-door. One gave away New Testaments to the Muslem Tatars in their own language.

The church planter who dropped out of the program and later came back had moved away from his fortune-telling mother to live in a different village. He still hadn't made much headway but worked on building relationships.

Each reported how many hours they had put in, until it was Ivan's turn. (Cory had provided chauffeur services at Ivan's wedding.) He said he hadn't put in even two hours a day and just couldn't discipline his life enough to give the kind of time he should. He wanted to drop out of the program.

He was already the pastor of a small church when he joined the training program. That year, his church of twenty members grew fifty percent when he baptized ten new believers. He saw no fruit, however, from his attempts to start a new group in a neighboring village.

Though Ivan said his problem was poor self-discipline, Cory thought fear affected him too. They stopped giving him a stipend, but Cory invited him to attend future church-planter gatherings for the fellowship and encouragement.

Pavel had the opposite problem of working too many hours. He had four groups in various villages and put in about sixty hours a week. That year, he baptized twenty people. Andre and Cory told him he needed to take a day off every week for time with his family.

Piotr, the Primorski pastor who sat in on the training, invited Cory to preach again at his church. This time, we took June. Though she had visited the Primorski church clinic, this was her first time to attend Sunday services there.

"I really liked the church service," she told Piotr during lunch at his house afterwards. Cory translated.

"I did too," I added. "I noticed you have many new people coming." That morning I counted 96 in attendance. "And I like the way you include the youth."

Piotr nodded. "The young man playing the electric guitar is not yet a believer," he said, "but he is talented and interested and comes to the meetings, so why not let him play?" That evening this teenager accepted Christ.

Piotr explained that the church board had set a goal of having at least one believing family in every apartment building in Primorski. That week, he printed up 3000 invitations to a Christmas program and gave them to church members to distribute in their neighborhoods.

He thought the church clinic provided a good outreach to the community and he went regularly to counsel patients. "It's a more efficient way to witness than if I go out and look for people to talk to." That summer he had baptized twenty-five people.

"You can't pour new wine into old wine skins," Andre and Stefan said often, referring to old churches and the need for new church plants.

We were surprised, therefore, by the response of the established churches to the church planters training program. Piotr was just one of four pastors who had attended the training program regularly and adopted a more outreach-oriented philosophy of ministry.

The church planters also generated vision at their home churches. When called upon to preach, they passed along the teaching they had heard in the training program. When they met together in their regional support groups every week, other Christians joined them. These had caught the vision and wanted to help with evangelism.

Several pastors urged Andre and Cory to train their congregations in evangelism. Starting in January, they began holding monthly seminars in four regions of Eastern Crimea: Nizhnigorsk, Sudak, Kerch, and Primorski. They also went to Sevastopol on the west side of Crimea.

Besides mobilizing churches for evangelism, they hoped to use the seminars to nurture and screen future church planters. They planned to cover topics like God's heart for reaching the lost, basic doctrines of the Bible, how to evangelize, and how to live a victorious Christian life.

Though the church planters program had the eager support of most churches in Eastern Crimea, the leader in Feodosia wasn't so enthusiastic. When Andre preached, "we are saved by grace," Igor rebuked him for not teaching "the whole Gospel." Igor stopped asking Cory to preach after he spoke about multiplication and church planting. Cory decided to spend more time with churches that welcomed his contribution.

With Cory gone more, the girls and I enjoyed June's companionship. We took advantage of nice weather one day in February and arranged to meet at a halfway point along the beach. Russian tourists paid admission to this sandy beach during the summer, but in the winter we had it to ourselves for free.

Janelle and Alicia made sand castles while June and I sat in the sun, jabbered, and munched on sunflower seeds. I had bought these, Ukraine's most common snack food, from a woman sitting at a street corner.

June talked about her work at the clinic and said, "It seems like people cry so easily here. Why is that?"

"I think it's because they aren't used to being treated kindly." I told her about "the weeping widow" in our apartment building who cried almost every time I spoke with her.

Tatiana, who translated for June, had told me June treated patients differently than the typical Russian doctor or nurse. She spoke kindly to them and explained what she was doing and why.

I had heard many horror stories about harsh doctors and nurses. "What are you moaning for? Of course it hurts, what do you expect!" And to a woman in delivery, "You should have thought about this when you got pregnant."

The two Christian doctors at the church clinic showed more kindness and prayed with their patients. June hoped to eventually teach them about wound care, her specialty in the U.S.

Janelle and Alicia used our sunflower hulls as little people to populate their sand castle. We found a discarded plastic pop bottle and collected sea water for the moat, then walked June to her apartment.

It was a little after dark when we took the bus back home. "I think it's scary to walk after dark," Janelle said when we got off the bus. "I'm afraid I'll step in some poo poo."

Living in Ukraine gave me a greater appreciation for America's leash laws and for the anti-dog-doo signs I'd seen in Europe.

June often used her free days to make the girls feel special. As Easter approached, she invited them to her house to work on a top-secret project: making Easter cards for Mom and Dad. When June brought them home again, they held several mangy-looking feathers in each fist. They had found them while walking home and thought the feathers helped them fly.

Alicia said excitedly, "With these feathers, I flied over a ditch."

"You mean you jumped over the ditch?" I asked.

"No Mommy, I flied, I really did!"

June told me about her dinner preparations. "I made several lengthwise cuts in half of each hotdog before cooking them so the cut strips curled up. I went and told the girls, 'I put hotdogs in to cook, but they turned into octopus! Come and see!'"

Janelle took over the story from here. "When she said the hotdogs turned into octopuses, my eyes got really big like THIS. And when I was going to the kitchen, I was thinking, 'Oh NO! Now we aren't going to have ANYTHING to eat.'"

Janelle and Alicia liked those octopus after all.

When the church planters gathered for their monthly meeting in March, Cory asked each to talk about their goals for the future. He wanted to encourage initiative, since the leaders couldn't stand over the church planters and direct their every move.

Of the eleven, only two could state a clear plan for their work. The idea of setting goals was a hard concept for most to grasp. They had grown up in a society where people at the top set the agenda and everyone else was supposed to wait for orders.

People also need stability in order to set goals. Many Americans feel they are "masters of their own destiny," but our country has had peace and prosperity for a long time. Those living in countries with frequent political and economic upheaval find goal setting more difficult.

Though poor at planning, most church planters had successfully started small groups and remained busy with evangelism. Ivan, who had dropped out discouraged two months earlier, now led a group of ten new believers in a neighboring village. An English teacher in his church had shared her faith with other teachers and they wanted to study the Bible.

This teacher was the one who brought her daughter to meet me three years earlier, and I fed them leftover borscht after church. Besides reaching out to her colleagues, she taught the Bible to children through several Good News Clubs.

In spite of several positive reports, Cory came home frustrated. He thought they made a mistake in taking back the one with the fortune-telling mother who dropped out of the program and later returned.

"He has a bad attitude most of the time, and there is another guy who also has a lot of excuses for not getting anything done," he said. As parents and teachers know, it's not the ones who do well who consume the most energy, but the ones who don't.

Cory explained, "After someone is part of the group, though, you don't want to give up on him. I still think these two have the ability to do the work. We told them to spend a couple weeks with Pavel. Maybe they can learn from his example."

- 28 -
Growing in Grace

My sister Linda wrote that the two boys she adopted from Ukraine made a delightful addition to the family. They were growing and healthy.

Arlene, my other sister, wrote, "Our application to adopt from Ukraine was approved!" She and her husband, Rob, had two children, but after several miscarriages, they decided to pursue adoption. Meanwhile, she discovered she was pregnant again and received treatment for the rare condition that caused the previous miscarriages. Nevertheless, they still wanted to adopt.

It seemed adoption was the only way I could get family members to visit, so I was happy to assist. I also figured that if I didn't accomplish anything else in Ukraine, at least I could help make a long-term difference in the lives of these adopted children.

I packed our bags and Cory took the girls and me to Simferopol, to an empty apartment rented for another missionary who hadn't yet arrived. I would cook while Rob and Arlene pursued stamps and signatures for the next three weeks. Janelle and Alicia made new friends: two little American boys who lived in the same apartment building. I, too, enjoyed the fellowship of other Americans at a women's Bible study for missionaries.

Rob and Arlene chose a seventeen-month old boy and considered another: a fourteen-month old boy weighing less than twelve pounds. His birth weight had been normal, but he was sick most of his first year.

They held this tiny child who was so weak he could not sit unassisted. His bright eyes met theirs. They faced a decision: adopt just one or take this second boy as well? When thinking rationally, just one seemed sufficient but that answer gave them no peace.

"We prayed about it last night," Arlene said the next morning. "We believe both of them belong to us."

Many people had told us, "I could never do what you do." I felt the same about Rob and Arlene's decision, since they would soon have five children age five and under. I felt great respect for their desire to give a hope and a future to these children, but could I do it? I don't know.

God doesn't call everyone to be missionaries, nor does He call everyone to take in orphans. God gives us the grace to do what He has called us to do, and whatever it is, we are to grow in godliness.

While doing my homework for the women's Bible study, I came across 1 Timothy 4:7: "Train yourself to be godly" (NIV). Godliness doesn't come naturally. Spiritual training, like physical exercise, requires diligence and self-denial, but gives strength and stamina.

Different athletes—swimmers, football players, and figure skaters—have different strengths; Christians have diverse abilities too. Whatever our gift, we have room for growth in godliness. We all must step out in obedience, deny selfish inclinations, and trust God with whatever lies down the road.

While Rob and Arlene pushed adoption papers, Janelle and Alicia played with the two little American boys who lived upstairs. On our walk through a park with them one day, the children stopped to "fish" from a stream using weeping willow branches.

"Mama, would you tie a piece of grass on my stick?" Alicia asked. "Isaac says the fish eat grass." I saw lots of garbage in the stream but no fish.

We lived near "Children's Park," the site of a small amusement park. There, the girls rode a rusty roller coaster several times and an ancient Ferris wheel. We also visited the small zoo at the park.

I felt sorry for the skinny animals in their dirty little cages. We took bread to feed the ducks and swans but ended up feeding the bears, goats, guinea pigs, and a camel. The wolves jumped in the air trying to catch small pieces of bread we tossed into their cage.

Rob and Arlene finally adopted their boys and brought them to the apartment for two nights. The boys were so light, Janelle and Alicia could easily carry them. They had good appetites though.

Growth is a normal part of being alive and healthy," Cory told church members assembled for an evangelism seminar. Andre and Cory continued to give monthly seminars in five regions of Crimea. About 300 to 350 people attended these each month.

Churches hosting the seminars demonstrated their commitment to evangelism by setting goals for new church plants. The believers in Nizhnigorsk had already started fifteen cell-groups in fourteen villages. This included eight groups led by church planters and seven led by other church members. They set a goal of starting churches in fourteen additional towns.

Board meetings were more like evangelism committee meetings, since the elders all helped with church planting or evangelism. The congregation of 150 members, plus visitors, burst the seams of the house where they held services. Though in the middle of a building program, the council decided they must not sacrifice evangelism for a building. Therefore, church members worked on construction just one day a week, on a rotating schedule, so they could continue with outreach activities.

The Sudak church had cell-groups in four villages and targeted ten more places for church plants. The Primorski congregation started new churches in two towns the previous year and selected four more sites. Kerch had three new churches and wanted to start four or five more. These villages with new groups and those targeted for church plants typically had 2,000 to 15,000 people. Most had no previous church at all.

Late in May, Cory came home encouraged from meeting with the church planters. All but one had started a cell-group. In fact, they had started eighteen groups with a total attendance of around 260 people. These figures didn't include two preexisting, growing churches pastored by two church planters.

Pavel worked with six groups in five villages. He started the last two with the help of new believers from his other groups. He mentored twelve young men, new Christians. He met with them weekly and they helped him with evangelism. One disciple led Pavel's newest group.

Pavel's success gave the clearest picture for what we hoped would happen: a church planting movement where group leaders could successfully train others to start even more groups. Though we rejoiced with what God had done through him, Cory and the other leaders had told Pavel not to work so hard.

Pavel reported, "I asked my men to pray I could clear one day a week to stay home with my family. I didn't think I could do it, but I got sick and had to stay in bed for three days. I never saw my guys the whole time and asked them later what happened. They were so busy with ministry, they didn't even miss me! I saw my pride and realized I had been trusting in my own strength."

One church planter set a goal of talking to 300 people one-on-one about Christ during the month of May. He made it to 135. Instead of ten people a day, he spoke to four or five. One started a "volleyball outreach" to get to know teens and young adults. Others continued to show Christian films and evangelize door-to-door. The two men sent to observe Pavel reported that though they had been reluctant to go, the experience changed their perspective on ministry and how to relate to people.

June rode the bus directly from the Primorski church clinic to our apartment one afternoon late in May. "I'm so excited, I just have to tell you what happened today," she said. That afternoon she led a woman to Christ, or was it Tatiana who did it?

The woman reeked of alcohol and looked depressed when she came to the clinic. A Christian friend had brought her there for counseling.

"June, would you talk to her?" the doctor asked.

Tatiana translated as the woman poured out her story. Her husband had died of a heart attack in February, and then her brother died two weeks later. She sank into depression and one drinking binge led to another. Friends coming to comfort her brought more alcohol. The woman hadn't gone to work, since she couldn't function when she was drunk. Her debts piled up.

As June listened to this woman's problems, she wasn't quite sure what to say. Tatiana, however, had just spent a week translating for a Christian counselor from Alabama. She gently coached June, "Lynn would tell her this…"

"Go ahead and tell her," June said.

Tatiana proceeded to give the woman the kind of advice she had been translating all week. She even quoted Bible references. The woman prayed, asking God for a new start.

"You could see the change come over her," June told me. "Her face went from being etched with fear and depression to having a glow. Her eyes shone with new hope."

June invited the woman to come back Friday for a follow-up visit. When Friday rolled around, the woman came, dressed up and smiling. She had been reading the Bible, praying, and staying sober. She had attended Bible Study on Wednesday and said she would go to church on Sunday.

Though not a believer in the official sense, Tatiana was rooting for the Christians. She seemed close to joining them, but said her husband wasn't ready and she thought they should make that step together. Still, she went home and told her husband the good things these Christians were doing.

In early summer, Cory visited several groups started by church planters. Forty-five people came to a group Leonid had started only three months earlier. The evening began at 5:00 with a pre-baptism study for fourteen people who had accepted Christ. At 6:00, thirty-one more came for tea, conversation, singing, and a short scripture reading.

They took turns introducing themselves and told when they had accepted Christ. Only three or four had been Christians longer than two years; most had repented within the past few months. A few had not yet made that step.

During his training, Leonid had asked the same questions repeatedly and was slow to see any ministry results. Leaders had encouraged church planters to start fellowship groups.

"But what do you DO with the group?" Leonid asked.

Have fellowship.

"But what is fellowship?"

The teachers tried to demonstrate through evenings dedicated to singing, conversation, tea, and a short Bible reading. Leonid finally discovered for himself the effectiveness of fellowship groups in reaching people.

As we finished dinner one evening, the phone rang. It was Sergei. "I need some advice," he told Cory. Fifty people from the Nizhnigorsk region wanted to be baptized and he felt unsettled about it. He was young, just 25, and inexperienced in his new role as pastor of the Nizhnigorsk church.

The problem, Sergei said, was that over half of those wanting baptism had been involved in the occult. Traditionally, the church did not give baptism until converts demonstrated their commitment through a changed lifestyle. Some were still dealing with leftover baggage.

"Change won't be easy for many of them," Cory said. "The enemy won't let go so easily. Still, they want to be free. Go ahead and baptize them, but continue to work with them." He suggested some resources.

Several weeks later, we attended the baptism at a canal that ran through the Crimean steppe. Thirty-two believers came for immersion. Eighteen more planned to take the plunge the following month.

When I asked Janelle and Alicia if they wanted to go, they responded with an enthusiastic "YES!"

I explained, "Remember how Daddy was teaching men how to tell other people about Jesus? All those people getting baptized want to follow Jesus now."

Janelle exclaimed, "Good job, Daddy!" They could finally see some results of our decision to live in Ukraine and an answer to their many prayers "for the people who don't know Jesus."

"Do you know what baptism means?" I asked.

"Yes," Alicia replied. "That's like saying you want to marry Jesus."

The new Christians dressed in white robes. Church members sang and prayed on the shores of the canal. Sergei gave a short scripture lesson, and then church planters Pavel and Leonid helped Sergei baptize the new believers.

Leonid's wife, Tamara, stood beside me. "It's such a blessing to see people starting to come to the Lord," she said. "We went through a crisis of faith when we didn't see any results for so long."

"So many people still don't know God," said Vera, Pavel's wife. "Our life was awful when we didn't follow Christ. I wasted so many years before I finally repented. Pavel was in the mafia and was terrible. He even threatened to kill me. I was baptized on October third and he repented on October fourth. Praise God. Now he is baptizing other people."

I watched Pavel dunk another young man under the water. He helped him up, then gave him a bear hug and a "holy kiss." God was changing one life at a time. There was hope for Ukraine.

All church planters eventually started cell-groups

- 29 -
Reap with Rejoicing

Our final summer passed quickly. A large medical and evangelism team from North Carolina visited for two weeks to work at the Primorski church clinic and in villages with our church planters.

Cory left home early each day and came back late, but I got a few details out of him. He said the medical outreach had done much to create good will in the villages and the medical personnel had been swamped. He saw people leaving the clinics with tears in their eyes, grateful and surprised the treatment was free. At evangelistic services held outside, many indicated that they wanted to follow Christ.

A group from Wichita followed this team; some sang and preached in villages where church planters worked. Their open-air concerts attracted many. Church planters would provide follow-up.

Two women from Wichita helped Anya lead a camp at Stefan's church in Batalnaya. Anya had found her niche as the Sunday School teacher and then as camp director. She and Stefan were thrilled by the camp's success. Because the church in Batalnaya was so new, all the children came from non-Christian backgrounds, though twenty-five or so had attended Anya's Sunday School before. A manageable seventy to eighty children attended daily with about one-third of them Tatar, culturally Muslim.

Some of the Tatar kids said they wouldn't pray to Jesus, only to Allah. By the end of the week, they prayed to Jesus too and took their Bible-related craftwork home to show their parents.

Stefan said, "The camp was a great witness to the village. People were surprised how well we took care of their children."

About thirty parents attended the closing program, some of them Tatar.

We planned to leave Ukraine at the end of August for a ten-month fur-lough. June would live in our apartment while we were gone, so I gave her a tour of the kitchen and showed her how to operate our gas stove.

Janelle and Alicia gave June detailed instructions too: "Make sure you give Christopher (our parakeet) enough food so he won't die. Don't jump on the beds and you need to pick up the toys if you play with them. And *don't stomp*, the people downstairs won't like it."

A group of friends from church gathered outside our apartment to bid us farewell. They sent us off with love and tears. After we checked in at the airport, passport officials confiscated Cory's passport and kept it an hour to inspect his visa stamps. Fortunately our plane was late, and Cory got his passport back in time. Our only tears were tears of relief when our plane lifted off.

It would have been more difficult to leave if we didn't expect to see our friends again, but we felt as if we had left the battlefield. We prayed for comrades we left behind but it was nice to have a break.

On our first Sunday evening back, our home church in Klamath Falls asked us to give an informal update. During the question and answer portion, one woman asked, "Do you feel there is a cost to being a mis-sionary?" Cory thought I should answer that one.

I dove in, then tried to paddle to the surface again. Yes, there is a cost. Pressures brought stress to our family and marriage. We went without outside supports nearby. We muddled through times of wondering why we didn't see God's blessing—why we didn't feel "fulfilled" after doing what we thought God wanted us to do. Only later did we experience the truth that "those who sow in tears will reap with rejoicing." We might have given up too soon.

I learned what it means to "present your body as a living sacrifice" with the physical hardships. A women's conference I attended in Ukraine helped my perspective, with speaker Elizabeth Elliot who said that Jesus suffered, so why shouldn't we suffer too? This is the normal Christian life: to offer our lives as a sacrifice to Christ.

Afterward, I thought more about this woman's question and felt my answer was incomplete. Sure, there is a cost to being a missionary, but there is also a cost to being a parent. Every worthwhile undertaking has a price tag.

I don't want to focus on the cost so much I forget God's repayment plan. Jesus said, "I will never leave you nor forsake you." He promised those who leave father, mother, brother, sister, houses, and lands will gain them back many times over.

We saw God's faithfulness during furlough. I often met people who said, "I pray for you every day." We were surrounded by supportive fathers, mothers, brothers, and sisters. We had many houses and lands available to us.

We had time to refuel. We worshiped in English, read books, and met with friends. Janelle and Alicia learned to roller-skate and ride bikes. They went inner- tubing for the first time and discovered the library. Cory took the girls fishing. I attended a women's conference.

At the retreat, I walked along the lake before breakfast and took time to get things squared away with God. Coming back to America, I basked in His gracious gifts—but where was God in Ukraine? Often, I didn't feel particularly close to Him or feel He was being "nice" to me. Like the poem about the footprints in the sand, I saw only one set of footprints during the tough times. *Where were you when I needed you?* "That's when I carried you." That too is grace.

I recalled the story of Jonah. He preached in Nineveh and then sat under a vine that withered. He became upset. God rebuked him saying, you are so concerned about your own comforts and a silly vine but don't care about the 120,000 people in this great city who don't know their left hand from their right. *Jonah was a self-centered jerk*, I thought.

Then I saw myself. I didn't like living in Ukraine because of the lack of comforts—my vine had withered. I, too, cared more for a silly vine than I did for the multitudes. The fact that the people lived in such despair had been another item on my complaint list—it's depressing to live among such people.

I didn't love these people as God loves them. Jesus came and sacrificed because of His great love. Sacrifice without love dries up the bones. How do you get the love when you don't have it?

Our speaker at the women's retreat told about a set of siblings she and her husband had adopted. At one time, she'd thought of herself as someone with a great love for all children. The girl was so spiteful, however, she didn't love and couldn't love this child. Then she realized, "for this, Christ died." If she could do everything she should on her own, then Christ's sacrifice was unnecessary. She prayed God would give her His love for her daughter—and He did.

I left the retreat with a new excitement about our work in Ukraine. I felt privileged to serve God as a missionary, to participate with Him in His redemptive work in the world.

God *was* at work. Andre sent us regular updates during our furlough. "We counted around 1150 villages in Crimea," he wrote, "and if you remember, one goal of the church planting movement was to plant a church in every village, so that means there aren't many left—only 1100."

He said they felt intimidated by the number until they realized that even if all those villages had one church with 100 people, only five percent of Crimea's population would be saved.

"God wants *all* people to know Him," he wrote, "not just five percent. We understood that our goal of 1200 churches is reachable—it's not like jumping over the moon. We know the Lord will bless us in this, since it is His will. We don't know how to reach this goal, but it doesn't frighten us any more. We go forward, like we did the past two years when we could see only to the turn in the road. The Lord is leading us and in His time, He will show us the part that lies around the bend."

Andre presented his church-planting vision to a gathering of pastors from all over Crimea. They responded with enthusiasm and wanted to send men for training.

In December, they began a three-month course in evangelism for forty-five men and met two days every other week. After three months, they chose thirty for further training as church planters. These men were already active in evangelism and working to start small groups.

We went to Ukraine intending to focus on the Feodosia church, pouring our effort into one channel. We felt disappointed at first by a block in the river, but streams flowed around to water a much wider area. God has a way of doing immeasurably more than we can ask or think.

Cory received several job offers during our furlough, but they seemed like a step down. We've been ruined for the ordinary. We look forward to returning to Ukraine and seeing what God will do around the bend.

Afterword

I wrote Five Loaves and Two Bowls of Borscht to encourage perseverance when life or ministry is difficult. With the first edition now out of print, I offer this second edition, believing the lessons God taught us can still help others.

Our living conditions improved as we returned to Ukraine. A better economy led to more modern appliances and fewer power outages. A hot water heater and an automatic washing machine made life easier, but we still found fresh opportunities to lean on God.

During our first term, I never imagined we would stay in Ukraine for fifteen years. God sustained us each step of the way—through eviction from our new apartment, challenges in the ministry, and death of a colleague. *Steppes of Faith*, my next book, tells the rest of the story. It also includes faith-building stories of people we came to know and love.

Life anywhere includes challenge. We can follow God with confidence because He works in ways we cannot.

May God bless each reader with a bigger picture of His faithfulness.

Janice

Feedback on Five Loaves

It's so good to pick up a book and be able to relate so much to the story. Thank you for writing this book and for being so honest in it. – China

I found myself challenged and encouraged while reading your book. It served as a devotion book for me and I plan on reading it again for that purpose. – USA

I continue to think about your statement: "After I stopped fighting with God, life in Ukraine became more enjoyable. Sure, our water and electricity continued to go off. . . but I stopped looking for things to justify my discontent." Reading this helped me realize that's what I was doing. It's easy for me to look for things to justify my discontent.
Many more things stood out to me and ministered to my soul as I read. You are so real, and I think that's one reason so many missionaries find your writing refreshing and encouraging. – Indonesia

I love it for many reasons. You say stuff I have been struggling to express to others about what it is like to serve as a missionary overseas! Thanks for writing your experiences. Good reminder of why we do what we do. "For this. . .I have Jesus." – North Africa

I can relate to so much that you've written. We don't have the same physical hardships here – but it was the other issues I could relate to. Thank you for the book and for the Bible study. The Bible study is just excellent and God is using it to convict and transform me! – Italy

My ideas of living for Jesus have changed since I read this book. I now know how much of a gift knowing God really is. – USA

Bibliography

Gallit, Mark. "Is Persecution Good for the Church?" *Christianity Today,* May 1997.

Keane, Glen. *Adam Raccoon and the Race to Victory Mountain.* Elgin, IL: Chariot Books, 1993.

Lawrence, Brother, retold by Winter, David B. *Practicing the Presence of God.* Wheaton, IL: H. Shaw Publishers, 1991.

Marshall, Catherine. *Christy.* London: P. Davies, 1968.

Sheldon, Charles. *In His Steps.* Topeka, KS: Private Print, 1938.

Stevenson, Mary. "Footprints in the Sand."

Tucker, Ruth. *Guardians of the Great Commission.* Grand Rapids: Academie Books, 1988.

Other books by Janice Lemke:

Steppes of Faith:
Discovering God's Goodness in Ukraine

Finding Strength for the Journey:
A Bible Study Guide

Visit: www.purposepress.net

E-mail: purposepress@gmail.com

Ask about a discount rate for bulk orders.

CPSIA information can be obtained at www.ICGtesting.com
Printed in the USA
BVOW09s1230041214

377191BV00001B/4/P

9 780984 594955